The Angel and the Frog

Becoming Your Own Angel

A SPIRITUAL FABLE

SCP LIMITED
2700 St. Louis Avenue
Long Beach, CA 90806

ISBN 0-9623282-5-1
COPYRIGHT 1997

DEDICATION

To Kien Lam
A Vietnamese Angel who touched my life

The Angel and the Frog

Becoming Your Own Angel

A SPIRITUAL FABLE

FATHER **Leo Booth**

Foreword by
Gary Zukav

Table of Contents

Foreword
Gary Zukav

Spiritual growth does not begin until you have the courage to enter into relationships. It requires more than meditations, prayers and good wishes. Relationships are the proving grounds where the effects of intentions, conscious and unconscious, become known. Lack of relationship equals stagnation from the spiritual perspective.

The Angel and the Frog is about relationships — with fellow students in the Earth school and with nonphysical Friends. These are my terms. The characters in this book confront the same challenges that we face, with the same issues that we have: How to live lives of integrity while honoring the paths of others; how to see the roles that we play in the genesis of our own experiences; and how to recognize, incorporate and utilize our highest understandings.

These issues are not the substance of fable. They are becoming the core issues of every human as human evolution through the alignment of the personality with the soul replaces human evolution through the exploration of the physical world. The appearance of Angels in this book reflects the appearance of Angels in the lives of millions of humans. Angels are not new. The emerging ability of the entire human species to interact with them consciously is.

Every human endeavor is a collaboration. Five sensory humans — those that are limited to the perceptions of the five senses — cannot see this. Multisensory humans — those whose perception is expanding beyond the perceptual system of the five senses — can. We are all becoming multisensory.

In this book, Cedric, a frog, collaborates with an Angel, and this deeply affects his life and the lives of those around him. One by one, each of us is becoming conscious of collaboration with nonphysical Teachers, and this is changing our lives as radically as it changes Cedric's. Those changes are not identical. Some individuals open to new and previously unconsidered positive potential. Others close more tightly into old patterns of fear. The same thing is happening to us.

A great change is upon us. More accurately, within us. This change is beyond our ability to control, just as the sudden and unanticipated appearance of an Angel in Cedric's life is beyond Cedric's ability to control. Our only option — like Cedric's — is how to respond. *The Angel and the Frog* is about different responses. Cedric accepts and befriends the Angel. Are we doing the same? Cedric's Angel does not look like an Angel. Frequently, ours do not, either. Cedric finds his Angel in a pond. In folklore, myth, and dreams from antiquity to present, water is the element of emotions. Our Angels often speak to us in the same way — through our emotions. Are we listening?

Angels — nonphysical Teachers — see us more clearly than we see ourselves, concern themselves only with our spiritual development, and speak only the truth in ways that we can understand it. These are their values to us. They are spiritual Friends. They model the love that we are becoming. They partner with us in the ways that we are learning to partner with one another — as equals for the purpose of spiritual growth.

The Angel and the Frog is about collaboration with an Angel and the spiritual partnerships that develop as a result. It is about the deep emotional currents that move each of us, and the transformations that they offer. It is about becoming loving and grateful. It is also about the work that is necessary to do that.

Leo Booth was on the stage with me when I first shared publicly some of my early encounters with a nonphysical energy dynamic that called itself an Angel. It took me — a Harvard graduate, former Green Beret officer, and former popularizer of physics — many years to find the courage to do that. Because of this, Leo honored me by referring to me in *The Angel and the Frog* as one of the Big People who speaks with a senior Angel named "Genesis."

What Leo did not know when he wrote this book is that the name of "my" Angel is Genesis! So once again I feel the touch, metaphorically speaking, of my spiritual Friend.

I am grateful to Leo Booth for this beautiful collaboration. It is a book that I look forward to rereading many times, to myself, and to my grandchildren.

—Gary Zukav

Introduction

"Stretch!"

As this fiat burst from Jean Houston's lips, the seed of The Angel and the Frog quickened in my mind. It is fitting that this stirring should occur just then, for it happened during an extraordinary event called "Birthing the Universal Human."

Jean and I, along with Gary Zukav, Joan Borysenko, Barbara Marx Hubbard, Gay and Kathlyn Hendricks had been called by Rev. Mary Manin Morrissey to come together as the core faculty of the Society for the Universal Human. We would hold our first gathering in February 1996 at the Living Enrichment Center outside Portland, Oregon. Our purpose was to co-create a spiritual society preparing itself for the New Millennium. Beyond religions, politics and social mores, we affirmed and visualized a society of divinely impregnated humans. How would they think? What would they look like? How would they behave? Equally important, how would we involve the conference participants in our vision?

Most of the faculty were used to delivering lectures, workshops, psycho-drama, meditations, visualizations. Some had already begun enhancing their sessions with light, music, dance and color. Now we were all being exhorted to toss out our standard presentations, learn from each other and with each other in order to stimulate our creativity and bring the participants into the process.

"*Stretch!*" Jean challenged us to reach past our limits and push, push for... *more.* Take that leap of faith. Risk. Move into the shaping of the human drama. STRETCH. Then stretch again. So instead of presenting the workshop I'd so carefully prepared, with overheads and experiential exercises and process questions, I found myself on-stage improvising a little drama. Knowing my admiration for Oscar Wilde, Jean set the scene. I would portray Oscar Wilde during his imprisonment. There all similarity to history vanished, for in our drama, Oscar is visited by an angel from the future: Joan Borysenko. I cannot tell you what we did. For as we spun our little fable, the memory of a dream I'd had months earlier popped into my head.

I rarely remember my dreams, and when I do, I generally don't think to tell people what I've dreamt. But this one was so unusual, I came bounding into my office at Spiritual Concepts all excited to share my dream. It was November 1995. My conference coordinator, Sharon Shaw and Kate Russell, my editor, were busy getting work done before our holiday hiatus. I interrupted them: "Stop everything! I've dreamt my next book! Come and listen to this dream!" It was the most amazingly vivid dream I've ever had. A little frog named Cedric and a dripping-wet angel named Christine were having a profound conversation about a spiritual process, and having adventures along the way.

As so often happens in dreams, while I remembered with clarity how the Angel and the Frog looked like adorable Disney cartoon characters, I could not remember their profound and earth-shaking conversation. Nevertheless, I knew with a certainty that my next book would be a work of fiction, and its central characters would be the Angel, Christine and Cedric, the Frog. Now if I could just remember the plot! I immediately set out to try to write it, and got stuck. Then I got busy with the holidays, and a heavy workshop schedule in January. The frog and the angel got buried under the pressures of workshops, church duties, and preparing for the 10-day Universal Human event in February 1996.

Perhaps they were not so much buried as planted. Beneath my busy surface, the idea continued to germinate. Now, under the blazing sun of this extraordinary event, in the glare of a spotlight on a stage, the seed ripened and began to grow in earnest. Pieces fell into place: it would be a fable about angels and animals, archangels and even THE ONE WHO KNOWS, all struggling to move into the spiritual Process. Into the More.

How do I understand, let alone explain, the stretch from a bottle of gin to a frog named Cedric. In my drinking days, I was not visited by pink elephants or talking frogs. Yet, there is a connection. A continuum. Sometimes, reality is stranger than fiction. Nothing that follows in this book is more incredulous, fantastic or unimaginable than my own personal journey from being an alcoholic English priest to being a nationally known spiritual motivator and author, living in Los

Angeles, lecturing and conducting workshops on developing a new, co-creative relationship with God.

In the early days of my recovery, people would say, "Remember to thank your Guardian Angel before you go to sleep!" The message was clear: you are sober because some divine entity took care of you. However, I never believed that was the full story. My recovery involved *me*. At the beginning of my treatment in 1977, I knew subconsciously I needed to become my own angel. I needed to give my hopes and dreams feet. But how do you say this without appearing ungrateful to a Higher Power? How do I balance a belief in a loving God and personal responsibility? The decision I made in 1977 to embrace my recovery put me on the path that led to Tunbridge Pond and *The Angel and the Frog*.

And so began what I call in this book the discovering of the Spiritual Principles of Insight, Wisdom and Harmony. The Process. My first three books, *Spirituality and Recovery*, *Say Yes To Life*, and *Meditations For Compulsive People* were published by Health Communications. They introduced the idea that spirituality and religion are not the same. Religion is almost an accident of birth, like sex and race. Most people are born into whatever religion their parents espouse. So we are born Catholic, Baptist, Episcopal, Hindu, Moslem, Jewish. Healthy spirituality, being positive and creative, brings religion alive. Working primarily with alcoholics and other addictive problems, I tried to show how living a positive, creative life could help maintain a lasting, happy recovery.

But I immediately began running into a wall. In the late 1980's, the televangelist scandals erupted, exposing the sick underbelly of unhealthy religion. Perhaps its prominence in the news made it safe for people to express their anger and hurt at God. At a support group meeting, I heard someone jokingly say, "I'm a recovering Catholic." Everyone in the room roared with laughter. It was the laughter that is born of shared pain.

In that moment, I realized the wall I kept hitting was the primal and universal pain of religious abuse. Beneath the laughter, that pain screamed to be healed. Obviously, being shamed or disempowered in the name of God is not unique to Catholicism. Nor is fundamentalism the province of Baptists and Pentecostals. At that same time, warring Shiites and fanatical Tamils bloodied the Middle East. It seemed there was no corner of the world in which people were not dying or suffering in the name of a God we were emphatically told is just and loving.

Although there were hundreds of books dealing with dysfunctional families and the addictive society, few dared to explore how religion could be used addictively. Several books chronicled the televangelist scandals. None called the problem religious addiction, nor was its practice labeled religious abuse. This led me to write the controversial book, *When God Becomes a Drug*, published by Tarcher in 1991. In tackling this taboo topic, I stretched from discussing the excitement and energy of spirituality to walking in the valley of the shadow of religious addiction and abuse. For three years, I focused almost exclusively on this dark pain, the rotting underside of religion. I met scores of people who had gruesomely painful stories of sexual abuse and betrayal in the name of God. I heard from hundreds of others who all had the same lament: How could they be expected to turn their lives over to a God who made them feel helpless and guilty?

Someone called my office and complained, "Nobody ever told me how to have a grown-up relationship with God!" This cry became the next milepost in my stretch, and the basis for my book, *The*

God Game — It's Your Move, published by Stillpoint in 1994. It was the answer to the cries of those who wandered in the valley of the Shadow, seeking to somehow find a whole and happy relationship with God. The refugees from religion wanted to come home, but how to make religion safe? I stretched some more, confronting my own beliefs about religion, the role of the clergy, the language of liturgy. In this stretch, I discovered a new understanding of spirituality. We don't "get" spiritual through religion and ritual. We are created spiritual, in the Mental, Physical and Emotional gifts God bestowed within us. Unhealthy religious messages and traumatic life experiences disconnect us from that spiritual power. It's time to plug in, reconnect and grow up in our relationship with God.

The God Game challenged the religious and non-religious alike to move into new territory, to be willing to understand the context of scripture and interpret it, rewrite prayers and psalms to reflect the empowered, co-creative relationship with God. *The God Game* affirmed and validated that religious abuse was real. Then it invited the wounded to become their own healers.

Wow! This has been some stretch. *The Angel and the Frog* is the culmination of the journey that has taken me out of a rigid obedience to the form of religion, to a glorious empowerment and renewed faith in what it means to be divinely human. In an age that seeks spiritual answers from agents outside the human condition, this book challenges us to connect with the divine spark that burns in each of us. Truly, we are angels in the dirt!

Tunbridge Pond

It all began as just another ordinary day. From behind the clouds the sun attempted to attract our attention, but with a modicum of success. The grey clouds squeezed out an occasional raindrop upon the still pond and Betty, Alice and Irma, the chickens that belonged to Olde Stable Farm, could be heard arguing and shouting in the distance. The wind purred rather than blew, and Cedric, the hero of this story, if there really is a hero in life, was sitting by the side of Tunbridge Pond looking sad and empty. His eyes just stared. The stare of boredom. The stare of nothingness. His eyes just stared — and occasionally blinked. The thrill of living had departed from this little frog and only the shadow of existence remained.

Cedric was probably the most popular animal at Olde Stable Farm. His popularity rested in his genuine kindness. He did not have a wicked bone in his amphibian body. When the other animals had a problem, needed something done, felt sad, Cedric appeared as the frog in shining armour. He quickly moved beyond resentments and lived forgiveness.

Sure, he was known to be rather dramatic, often misquoting from literature or confusing and mispronouncing famous characters in history. Putting this aside, he was loved and respected by all the resident animals. Nevertheless, as often happens in life, Cedric felt that life had become meaningless, dull and boring. Why? He didn't know.

Cedric had just returned from a busy morning helping some of the animals that lived at Olde Stable farm. Betsy, the resident pig, had needed some cleaning done at the Sty. Cedric often helped clean out the dirty straw, replacing it with fresh straw to make up her bed.

Betsy was so huge, and lazy. She rarely moved except on cleaning day, which incidentally was any day that the animals took it upon themselves to clean her up. Betsy's only real interest in life was food. She lived to eat. She had become the comic caricature associated with pigs: an eater. A few senior residents of Olde Stable Farm remembered her as a piglet. She was the runt of the litter, skinny, ugly and unwanted. As a newborn, she had to fight her brothers and sisters to get any milk; even Rosey, her mother, seemed to have little time for poor Betsy. Her early childhood was spent fighting for food. It had become her security blanket.

Cedric escaped his boredom and feeling of hopelessness as he dragged out the smelly straw replacing it with fresh.

"See how beautiful your bed looks now, Betsy. I'd much rather stay here and take a nap with you than pick up the eggs for Mrs. Ramsbottom from the chickens."

"Stop fussing, Cedric," breathed Betsy, as she slowly awakened from her morning nap. "Nothing pleases you more than doing jobs and errands for your friends. You know you love to deliver the eggs to our revered owl. Indeed, you will use any excuse to hop over and see Mrs. Ramsbottom. It's what you like to do. I declare that you love hoppin' as much as I love sittin'. If we could create children, which would take a Rain-God miracle, maybe, just maybe, they would be half-way balanced!"

This sighed remark from Betsy, who was ever so lethargic in her speech, made Cedric smile.

"Well, now I'm off to get the eggs from Alice, Betty and Irma. I can hear their cluckings so they can't be too far away. As the Greeks would say, "Chow.""

As Cedric hopped over to see the chickens, he could see Chandu and Chico, the two burmese cats, talking with Old John the mule. He couldn't help but think about Betsy's remark. He really did enjoy helping his friends at Olde Stable Farm, and he'd noticed that his gloom and boredom mostly came when he was alone. He didn't enjoy his own company very much.

That's why he loved reading about the famous characters of history and literature: he could escape, if only for a short time, into their lives. They seemed so full of life, surrounded by adventure. Truth to tell, although he'd never said this to any of the animals, he didn't really know who he was or what he needed in life to make himself happy. His happiness, for the moment, came in helping others.

As Cedric approached the chickens, he heard Alice remark to Betty and Irma, "Here comes the hopping delivery frog. Mrs. Ramsbottom's pet."

Betty and Irma clucked in agreement, their heads bobbing and darting in all directions. Cedric felt dizzy just looking at them.

"I heard that. I heard what you just said. That's a toad of a remark. I'm not anybody's pet, but I do like to help. What's wrong with that? Why are you always clucking nasty things about your neighbors? Gossip, gossip, gossip. One day it will all catch up to you." Looking at Betty and Irma, he said, "Mark my words. Remember what the great philosopher William Snakespit said: 'The evil that we cluck lives after us; the good is buried with the seed.' "

"We never said a word --word -- word" said Alice, reverberating through Betty and Irma. Betty scratched her way into the conversation, saying, "We only said, 'Here comes the happy frog, a dear friend of Mrs. Ramsbottom.' "

Irma clucked at the same time, "The owl who knows everything!"

"If she knows everything, and she certainly seems to know most things, she will know what you really said!" Cedric blinked in amazement at the brilliance of his remark. The three chickens blinked back, not knowing what to cluck. It was a blinking moment that nobody knew how to break. Cedric and the chickens just stared at each other.

At that moment, a furry tail smashed into Alice's beak and bowled her over into the other chickens. A paw flipped the side of Cedric and threw him into the egg basket. Fortunately, he was too light to do any damage to the eggs, but he felt shaken up.

"Toby!" Cedric screamed. "Watch where you direct that furry rudder you call a tail. Look at the havoc you've caused!"

"Sorry. Sorry," Toby growled in the distance. "I'm going somewhere."

"One day I'll give that dog a piece of my mind," said Cedric.

Betty, Alice and Irma were still in shock, showered by their own feathers as they staggered to their feet.

"One day ... One day... One day..." they said in unison. "He'll run into a truck. That will stop him."

"May the Rain-God prevent such a tragedy," said Cedric.

Alice continued. "That's the only thing that will teach that flying dog a lesson. No animal is safe when that dog is going somewhere ... and he's always going somewhere!"

"I know," sighed Cedric. His gloom was descending and he knew he needed to move from the negativity that surrounded the chickens. He felt that he would cheer up if he got to see Mrs. Ramsbottom. Just being in her presence he had found to be a tonic.

"I'll pull this egg basket gently, so as not to damage any eggs. Wouldn't do to deliver broken eggs to Mrs. Ramsbottom."

"No. No. No," smirked the chickens. "It would be a tragedy for Mrs. Ramsbottom to be given broken eggs.

Scratching, Alice clucked, "Perish the thought!"

Cedric knew what they were doing, but felt it better not to argue. The chickens seemed to enjoy creating arguments. Better for him to continue his journey.

He put the basket under his chin and pulled it tight. Slowly, it began to slide along as Cedric hopped in the direction of Tunbridge Pond.

"Mrs. Ramsbottom! *Hoo. Hoo.* I say, Mrs. Ramsbottom!" Cedric announced his arrival.

"Stop that hoo-hoo-hoo-ing, Cedric! It's silly. And it doesn't mean anything. Would you like me to call you by imitating your frog voice and hollering *rib-bet, rib-bet*? So silly."

"Oh, no," said Cedric. "Is that how frogs sound to owls?"

"Something like that. Anyway, it's all rather silly. Just call me Mrs. Ramsbottom. In any case, I knew you were on your way after visiting those disgusting chickens."

"You'll never guess what they clucked," moaned Cedric. "They clucked..."

"Stop! No gossip. You only continue their madness," said Mrs. Ramsbottom. "I know what they were clucking about. Jealousy. Pride. It all goes back to the beginning of time. Sometimes, it seems like we take two hops forward and three hops back... I fear we've not heard the last of their madness. I'm so pleased that Toby got them with his tail. Right in the beak. A storm of feathers all over the place."

"Yes, yes," said Cedric. But how did you know? You couldn't possibly have seen what happened from your branch. How did you know?"

"Because I knew. I just know things," said Mrs. Ramsbottom. "I'm an owl. I'm supposed to know what goes on. That's my job. I'm sure it will all be revealed in time. I feel it in these old bones. And believe me, they are very old.... Now. The eggs. Ahh, beautiful. You see, Cedric, even chickens can do some things right! I'll eat a fresh egg for supper. Thank you so much!"

"It's no trouble. I like doing things for you. In fact, I've been thinking. I'm really only happy when I'm doing for others. I don't enjoy being by myself. I become... hop-less. Miserable. Gloomy. I don't know what I'd do if I didn't have friends. Timothy. Muriel. Snake. Chandu and Chico. Old John. Even Toby, if I could ever stop him running in all directions."

Mrs. Ramsbottom gave a long blink indicating a piece of wisdom was about to be birthed. "Friends are important. But *you* are essential. You love to quote from literature. Remember this sacred text: *What good does it do to gain the whole world and lose your own soul?*

"Cedric, you really don't appreciate who you are. You need something to wake you up."

"Where will I find this lesson?" asked Cedric.

"At home," blinked Mrs. Ramsbottom. "Home is where all important lessons are learned. Go back home and await your lesson."

So Cedric returned to his favorite place at the side of the pond after a satisfying morning helping his friends. Listening to the wind murmur through the trees, he could hear the echoing wisdom of Mrs. Ramsbottom: *Cedric, you don't appreciate who you really are.*

Sitting alone at the side of the pond, Cedric again began to experience the feeling of hop-lessness. He realized that the joy had gone out of his jump.

Dramatizing his melancholy, he pondered what William Snakespit said when he remarked to Napoleon:

"To be, or not to be: that is the answer."

He was definitely having a bout of the megrims and vapours. He could not put his webbed finger on what was causing this despondency and hop-lessness. Of course, the chickens and their gossiping tickle-tattle always got under his skin, even though they gossiped about everyone on the farm, including each other, so that was nothing new. Nobody had said anything particularly harsh or hurtful to him -- nothing that hadn't been said before. He couldn't think what could be the matter.

Perhaps he was missing his friend Snake. He realized that Snake had not been seen for weeks. Snake was always called 'Snake', and was always referred to as a 'he' although nobody, including Snake, knew for sure whether he was a he or a she. It was not so unusual for Snake to be away for a while, yet it added to the constant uncertainty and instability that existed for all the animals that lived around Tunbridge Pond. Animal life was living a day at a time — really it was more moment by moment. When animals disappeared or were not seen or heard from for weeks at a time it created the "not-knowing" fear that was not talked about, but all the animals felt. Death and disappearance were all part of the givenness of life at Tunbridge Pond.

Cedric missed not seeing Snake, but he did not feel that this was the reason for his gloom.

A possible factor for Cedric's sadness was that he had not been visited this week by Muriel, the pond hedgehog who was the nearest thing he had to a girlfriend in life, although their meetings were often a mixture of happiness and stress. Muriel wanted life to go in exactly the same way that she traveled, in straight lines. Muriel did not appreciate curves of any variety. No surprises. No detours. "Everything has a place and there is a place for everything." This was her creed. And it was enough.

Muriel had not been around this week either, but Cedric knew that this was not the cause of his melancholy. He said to himself, "As the song says, there is a time to live and a time to die. Perhaps there is also a time to be miserable. Maybe some animals are born to have miserable lives. Not everybody can be happy all the time. And some of us are rarely happy. Oh dear. To be sad because of some reason is understandable. To feel sad and to have no reason is plain stupid!

"But am I stupid?" he mused. "Is it me? I don't know what I'm doing to cause this sad feeling. If it is a sad feeling. Maybe hop-less is the stage before the feeling of miserable and sad. I don't know what it is. I don't even know if it's my fault. Maybe I'm the victim of some horrible spell put upon me by the Big People. The Big People lived beyond the hills that surround

Old Stable Farm. Oh dear, what should I do?" Again, for some moments he continued to stare blindly across the pond. He was one sad-looking little frog.

"I know what I'll do. I'll visit Mrs. Ramsbottom again, and ask her what she meant this morning by saying that I don't appreciate who I really am. Maybe she has a remedy for this hop-lessness. She usually has the solution for everything. Indeed, I've found that just talking to her is the solution."

He was just about to hop over to see Mrs. Ramsbottom when he heard a gentle plop in the middle of the pond. It was followed by a ripple of water that tickled his legs as they dangled against the cool banks. What could it be? Within seconds, a faint cry pierced the silence. "Help me! Help me!"

Cedric swam out into the Pond and past the old oak tree that spread her huge branches over the Pond, and there he saw... what did he see, spluttering out there in the water? Good gosh, it was the smallest, tiniest little Big Person he had ever seen. And she had the smallest little see-through wings that were flapping about in the Pond creating the tickle-ripple.

"Be still!" Cedric shouted. "Don't panic! I'm coming out to get you!"

Her voice was faintly audible to the frog. "Come quickly! My wings are soaking in the water and I'm beginning to sink. Oh dear, what a mess I'm in!"

Within seconds Cedric was next to her and he saw the most beautiful face and hair that he had ever seen — even though her face was wet and her hair disheveled. Her face radiated a glow and her hair had a golden sheen. She had a beautiful slender body covered in a white silk gown that he had seen Big People wear when they danced in the fields. But never had he seen a dress that sparkled like this one. Everything about this little Big Person was beautiful. Beautiful feet, beautiful hands, and the most gorgeous blue eyes. And everything was so very small and precious. He was just looking at her when he heard again the faint voice.

"Help me. I'm drowning!"

He arranged his little frog body so that she could climb on his back and he swam to the safety of the bank, beneath the oak branch that cast the shadow into which they reposed.

After they had rested for many minutes, Cedric felt that he had to find out who this beautiful creature was. "My name is Cedric. I'm a frog. I don't mean to be impertinent, but I have never seen anything like you before. I've lived at this Pond for seven years and I've seen all kinds of creatures that have passed through on their journeys, but never have I seen anything that even remotely resembles such a creature as yourself. Who are you?"

"Nice to meet you, Cedric." The creature took a deep breath and spoke in a voice that resembled music.

"My name is Christine. I'm really an angel in training. I've just returned from deep inside the Big Country helping a very special member of the Big People. His name is Gary Zukav. He has been guided and instructed by an angel who is ageless. He calls this angel-guide Genesis. I was sent from my home in Paradise to learn from this exceptional angel and believe me, there is so much to learn! My head is full of wisdom and prophecy.

"I've got my wings, as you can see, but I really need angel-experience. My wings and my multi-colored glow are great visuals to have but they are no substitute for creating connection. Indeed, the glow is dependent upon an energy connection having been made, that's what creates the color. This is what Genesis says, and he's usually right.

"Few understand that angels need to be trained, they need to study in order to spiritually grow. They don't start off knowing everything. I'm able to do many things, thanks to Genesis, but I'm not able to do one-hundredth of the things that Genesis does with a pull on his earring."

Cedric looked shocked.

"Yes, before you ask, Genesis wears an earring. He also has the raspiest voice of all the angels in the universe. It sounds like sandpaper being scratched against a stone surface. He says his voice is the embodiment of evolvement.

"Let me explain. When THE ONE WHO KNOWS—"

Cedric interjected, "Isn't he a famous character that Socrates wrote about?"

For a moment, bewilderment appeared on Christine's face. Then she realized that Cedric was trying to impress her, but he had gotten his characters confused.

"No, my dear Cedric. THE ONE WHO KNOWS is the energy that started everything. Now, where am I?"

"At Tunbridge Pond," Cedric eagerly reminded her.

"I mean where am I in the story. Yes, I've got it. When THE ONE WHO KNOWS created everything, it sounded like Genesis' voice — well, that's what Genesis says and it's best not to argue with him. Genesis is also multi-dimensional and multi-historical. Come to think of it, I'm the same. But I'm not talking about me at the moment. I'm talking about Genesis. He can be in more than one place or time zone simultaneously. You know he's around when you smell incense."

Cedric could not contain himself. "You mean the angelic spokesperson has an earring, speaks like sandpaper being scratched against a stone, and smells like incense? Wow! William Snakespit was right when he said to Romeo that there is more to heaven and earth than we can dream about. Wow! This is fantastic. I can't believe that all this is happening as we plod our weary way at Olde Stable Farm and Tunbridge Pond."

Cedric knew he was playing the role of an excited character who has just found a new friend. A special friend. An angel in training. Always his gloom and feeling of hop-lessness left when he was in good company. He began to feel happy as he talked with Christine.

Christine continued. "Yes, it's all very wonderful. Indeed, the knack to living the angelic life is existing permanently in the state of wonderment. And you don't need wings to live the life of an angel.

"However, I cannot emphasize this enough: Even angels, even Genesis, even THE ONE WHO KNOWS, are all evolving. Discovering. We're all part of The Process. Now, back to my story."

Suddenly, Cedric's nose started to twitch. A faint smell of incense tingled in the air. Christine's body began to glow with a pale yellow light. Genesis spoke so that only Christine could hear, and time stood still. The scratchiness of the voice never ceased to make Christine wince.

"Remember what I've told you, Christine. Don't preach. Don't be so long-winded. You'll put everybody to sleep. Remember to keep it simple. You are speaking to Cedric the frog, not Confucius. You are here for a reason. The reason is not clear to you yet, but give yourself time. I won't be too far away. Seek to teach The Process."

With that, Genesis was gone.

The Spiritual Principles

Christine took a moment to collect her thoughts. Cedric just stared at her. He was completely unaware that she had just had an encounter with her mentor, although there was still a sweet whiff of incense in the air.

Christine wondered whether she should be sharing what she knew about The Process so early in their meeting, but her impetuous spirit drove her on. She didn't want to preach; rather, she attempted to lead Cedric into The Process. She sensed he was eager to learn. It was no coincidence that this frog, Cedric, had saved her life. She tracked down her original point.

"Ah yes. I think I was telling you what I was doing with the Big People. Gary Zukav is an exceptional Big Person who is seeking to understand the Spiritual Principles that will help those who are becoming the seekers."

"Is it a new religion?" asked Cedric?

"Oh dear, no. The last thing that the Big People need is another religion. What the seekers are searching for is a spirituality that is beyond any one religion and yet it includes the best of all the great religions. Although religions have been around for many thousands of years, the majority of Big People don't really understand the Spiritual Principles that create Insight, Wisdom and Harmony.

"We enter The Process with Insight. That is when you see or recognize intuitively that things are more than they appear. It does not have to be complicated, but it is always profound. THE ONE WHO KNOWS is in everything if you have the eyes to see and the mind to understand.

"Wisdom follows Insight. It is the method we choose to communicate what we have understood. We can communicate with words, music, silence, touch, ritual… we communicate the More."

Cedric became excited. "What is the More?"

Christine glowed and Cedric felt a warmth in the pit of his tummy. "Harmony. Oneness. This is when we understand that all things are connected and there is a golden thread that joins everything to THE ONE WHO KNOWS. It is divine energy. So The Process is the interconnection of Insight, Wisdom, and Harmony.

"So many of the Big People read the Scriptures and practice their ceremonies, yet they miss the Spiritual

Principles that reside within each and every one of them. The Spiritual Principles are the fabric of common sense. Unfortunately it is not so common. Learning is the key to simplicity. The Big People have made discovering the Spiritual Principles so complicated over the centuries that everybody is confused about which religion is right.

"Genesis, the angel guide who is helping Gary Zukav, is teaching the principles of sacred simplicity. It's not really about what group you belong to or what particular ceremonies you practice or even which religious teacher you choose to follow— rather, it is about discovering the spiritual synchronicity that connects all the seekers of the Truth. The words synchronicity and spirituality seem to be the In-Words for the Big People at the present time."

Cedric hated to show his ignorance but he had to ask Christine a question. "What do you mean, *In-Words?*"

"Well, Big People are very funny when they become a group. At different times they get excited about a particular word or concept and it can last for quite some time. Then, for no apparent reason, the word or concept goes out of vogue. Big People easily get bored. So they rush out to find another word or phrase and eventually get tired of that one. What they don't seem to understand is that the Spiritual Principles can never

ever be captured by a word or phrase and so Big People need to search for the meaning *behind* the words or phrases. The Spiritual Principles never change. And they can never be contained in any one creed, scripture, word or phrase. The Spiritual Principles are always in the More. The More always exists beyond words or phrases.

"For the most part, Big People have become the prisoners of their own religious systems that they developed in their separateness. War and violence are conducted in the name of a particular belief creating insecurity, sadness and depression. The reason they are unhappy is because they are disconnected from the Spiritual Principles."

Cedric heard the words sadness and depression and he immediately thought about himself. Not ten minutes ago he was sitting by the Pond feeling... what? Disconnected. He didn't use that word, but when Christine said the unhappiness of the Big People was caused by being disconnected from the Sacred Principles, Cedric recognized the name of his feeling. He was unhappy because he was disconnected. Remembering what Mrs. Ramsbottom had said earlier in the day, maybe this was why he didn't appreciate himself. Christine, the angel who had literally dropped in on his life, might hold the key to *his* happiness. A frightening concept: Frogs may not be that different from Big People.

Cedric asked, "Are the Spiritual Principles just for angels and Big People or can anybody discover them and use them?"

Christine looked at Cedric with the warmest of smiles and as she did her face sparkled like her white shiny gown. "They are for *everyone*. They are for you. The Sacred Principles are a process to happiness and spiritual peace. It's not so much about what words, phrases or concepts that you believe. It's more a way of looking at life that creates Insight, Wisdom and Harmony. That's why I use the word process. You can use different words, practice different religions, or follow one or more spiritual teachers and yet still you are *in* The Process. The Spiritual Principles are a *Process*."

Cedric noticed that Christine's glow had diminished to a dull yellow. Although he did not fully understand how the glow reflected her energy, he did recognize that she was tired and needed to rest. He suggested that they slowly make their way to his home. His small cottage was not too far from the oak tree that highlighted the bend in the Pond. They could eat some small red berries and fresh grass. Already Cedric's lips were beginning to water. "Yummy. Berries and fresh grass." Then it occurred to him: Do angels eat frog food?

Christine knew what he was thinking. Knowing what other people are thinking and feeling is but one of the advantages of being an angel. However, sometimes angels choose to restrict their spiritual insights so that they can experience surprise and wonder in a new relationship. After all, it is not much fun being in a relationship if you always know what the other is thinking and feeling. Also, how are you able to evaluate intuition and the development of the Spiritual Principles? Christine was prepared to *limit* herself in her initial relationship with Cedric. She sensed that this angel-limitation was important.

Cedric asked aloud, "Do angels eat frog food?"

"Oh, yes. Because I'm an angel I am able to eat or not eat. I can live on the energy in the Universe and I can also choose to eat *anything* that any creature chooses to give me. The beauty of the food's taste is derived from the flowing generosity of the giver. Begin to understand this, Cedric. It is *you* who will make the food taste like honey for the gods!"

"But I hate honey! Frogs have never eaten honey and never will. Honey is bear food. Also, one bear told me he saw Big People eating honey on bread. Strange that Big People would eat bear food. Maybe that's why they are both big. Maybe if I eat honey I would be a big frog. Ugh! It might be nice to be big, but the thought of eating that sticky goo makes me sick!"

"No, Cedric," said Christine. "Honey does not make you big like a bear or the Big People. But you could eat honey if you felt the love of the creature who was giving you the honey. Generosity is transforming. It's been a very long time since I ate fresh grass but I know that your love and kindness will make it all taste wonderful. Everything you give me will be transformed by *your* generosity."

"Thank you, Christine. I think it was Aristonic, the Greek philosopher, who said that generosity is the pathway to happiness. That makes me feel very good. I feel wonderful in your presence. I don't feel hop-less anymore. I don't feel hop-less or empty. Christine, nothing has happened and yet I'm feeling exhilarated!"

"But Cedric, something *has* happened and *is* happening. We are *connecting*. You want to care for me and I am willing to trust your care. Relationship is two or more energies flowing together. Cedric, we are *making* relationship."

Cedric smiled. "You make it sound like a cake, Christine. 'Making' relationship!"

Christine's face glowed with a love that was beyond the physical. It came from a place deep within herself. Deep within the Universe. "It *is* like a cake, Cedric. We are making relationship with many ingredients. Look at where your hand is. It is resting on my arm. You are *touching* me. You are looking at me. The energy from your body is enveloping mine and I am responding. My glow is reflecting your energy and together we make connection. You care for me. You are concerned that I get rest. You want me to share your food. Share your home. Share your generosity."

"Then you will come home with me?" Cedric asked.

"Of course," Christine replied. "I want to visit your cottage. I want to express my gratitude to you. Cedric, you saved my life. I was drowning in the pond and you rescued me. For the short time that we have together we will both feed each other. And it will be special. Come, let me climb on your back and we will make the journey to your cottage slowly."

When they arrived at the cottage it was beginning to get dark. Many of Cedric's numerous relatives and friends were singing in harmony as the sun began its nightly immersion into Tunbridge Pond. All the animals that lived around the Pond were so proud and delighted that the Sun had chosen *their* pond to rest in each evening. The frogs and crickets created a wonderful orchestral background to the variety of songs sung by the neighborhood birds, all making up the music of the night.

Cedric opened the door and beckoned Christine to enter. He was ever the gentlefrog! It was a small cottage but was amply sufficient for Cedric's needs. Neatly arranged on the table were the berries and the fresh grass. Strange. Cedric had left the house that morning not wanting or expecting a friend to dine with him for dinner — and yet he had set the table for *two*. How very strange.

"Were you expecting a guest?" asked Christine.

"Certainly not. I don't know why I've set a place for two. It doesn't make sense. I know I wasn't expecting anybody for dinner. I always set a place for one. I don't know what I was thinking about."

"Stop there," said Christine authoritatively. "What were you thinking about? Tell me what was going through your mind this morning after you woke up from your sleep?"

"I was feeling hop-less. I was sad. Life was not making sense to me. I knew that I had friends. Muriel, Mrs. Ramsbottom, Snake, Timothy, Toby — even Alice, Betty and Irma — I had friends and yet I didn't feel... connected. I know that is your word, Christine, but truly that was how I felt. *Disconnected*."

"Tell me what was going through your mind this morning?" asked Christine.

"I felt something needed to happen. I wanted something to change. Things needed to change. I needed to do something different. I knew I needed help. I asked for help. I may have even prayed to the Rain-God to please let this inexplicable sadness lift from me.

"Yes, now I remember. I was setting the table for dinner when I said that prayer. I said it aloud: Please let this inexplicable sadness lift from me. But I'm not sure I expected anything..."

Christine interrupted. "Be careful what you pray for — it may arrive in the form of a very wet angel!"

"You don't mean that I was preparing for you? That I expected you? You're not telling me that I brought you into my life to get me out of the megrims and vapours, are you? Is that what you're telling me, Christine?"

"I'm not telling you anything. Let's not come to any conclusions at this point. Let's just observe what has happened and, if you like, thank the Rain-God.

"You asked for help.

"You set two places for dinner.

"And I'm here to be part of the solution, not add to the problem.

"Let me just share this with you, Cedric. I've been flying for over a hundred years and I've never misjudged my physical distance from water. And this day I get my wings caught in a gentle Pond water. No storm in sight. Maybe just a coincidence. Now let us eat. Bon appetite!"

Cedric was surprised at how wonderful the fresh grass and berries had tasted. He always enjoyed the mixture — but this time it tasted different. Sweeter. He couldn't help wondering what honey tasted like!

They were just about to rest on the carpet when somebody knocked at the door.

Christine said, "I think Muriel is at the door."

"How do you know it's Muriel? You don't even know Muriel. You've never seen Muriel. How could you possibly know that Muriel is knocking at my door? How?"

Christine had that love-glowing smile on her face. "You said that you had some friends: Muriel, Mrs. Ramsbottom... Snake... do you remember? Well, I connected the energy of the word M-U-R-I-E-L with the energy that is outside. This is not a trick, Cedric. It is putting The Process to work. Mingling Insight, Wisdom and Harmony to create intuition. And you can do the same."

"Nonsense! You don't expect me to believe that." Cedric opened the door. "Oh. Hello, Muriel. Yes, it really is Muriel. Do come in and meet a friend."

Muriel

When Muriel entered the cottage she bustled towards the table carrying a large supply of damp plant-roots. She was a plump hedgehog with neatly layered quills that nevertheless gave the message: Keep your distance. She scurried into the room, never moving her head, but her small beady eyes darted in all directions so that she seldom missed anything. In automatic movements she lifted her short arms and arranged the plant-roots neatly in the center of the table. Then, making an exact 45 degree turn, she looked towards Christine and blinked. And then blinked again.

Eventually she fired her questions. "Who are you? *What* are you? Where did you come from?" Muriel had a tendency to speak in threes.

"I'm an angel," Christine said with a smile. "I got my wings caught in the Pond and Cedric saved my life.

He then kindly invited me to join him for some supper and an evening's rest. You must be Muriel. I'm most happy to meet you."

"How do you know my name? I never met an angel before and until now I'm not sure I believed in them. Who told you my name is Muriel?"

"Cedric," Christine replied.

"But how did Cedric know I was knocking at his door? He opened the door and I walked in. Nothing was said. If something had been said, like, 'This is Muriel' I know I would have remembered. Nothing was said. My name was not mentioned. All very strange."

"Calm down," said Cedric. "Just take a moment to get your quills in order. You were in such a hurry to put the plant-roots down that you didn't hear me announce you at the door. I clearly said hello to you. That's more than you said to me. I also told you that I had company. But your mind was on one thing: your plant-roots, and you didn't hear a word I said. So just settle your quills and be nice."

Embarrassed, Muriel muttered under her breath, "Strange. That's what I say. Very strange."

"Yes," said Christine. "Life is strange. Much stranger than believing in angels!"

Muriel shrugged and barked, "Watch your backs! Strangers in the camp! Strangers, I say!"

"I'm not a stranger. I'm an angel. Actually, I don't believe in strangers. And do you know something, Muriel? Since I don't believe in strangers, I've never once met one!" Christine's flutelike voice was gentle, and she glowed a brighter yellow.

Although Muriel rarely warmed to strangers — the joke at Tunbridge Pond was that Muriel was six months old before she accepted her own family— her lips involuntarily started to curl in a faint smile. "I'm pleased to meet you. Do angels have names or do we call you Angel? In the same way that we call the snake, Snake?"

"My name is Christine." She turned to look at Cedric and then returned her gentle gaze upon Muriel. "And you are part of the reason that I am here."

Muriel looked at Christine with a mixture of shock and fear but then quickly turned her attention to Cedric. "I've brought you plant-roots to eat. Remember, I told you last week that I would be bringing you supper tonight. Your favourite. Plant-roots!"

This was not actually true. Cedric could eat plant-roots, indeed, he often ate plant-roots when Muriel came to visit, but this was because plant-roots were Muriel's favourite food and Muriel had a tendency to include everybody in her likes and dislikes. Muriel tended to think in black and white, good and bad, right and wrong, this way and not that way. Muriel expected the world to run according to her wishes, and that included everyone at Olde Stable Farm.

"I forgot you were bringing supper," Cedric sighed. "We've just finished eating berries and fresh grass. Mmmm. They were delicious. Would you like to try some, Muriel?"

"I've brought you plant-roots, Cedric." Muriel insisted. "And you can sit and eat them with your little angel friend. Of course, I will join you. I'm partial to the occasional plant-root!"

"I'm too full. Really I am!" exclaimed Cedric.

"Nonsense. We agreed. Tonight we eat plant-roots. They are sitting on the table waiting to be eaten. Let's eat!"

Perhaps because of the powerful glow he felt radiating from Christine, Cedric did something that he had never *ever* done before. He said *NO* to Muriel.

"Did I hear the word *NO*? Could it be that my friend, the frog, who I have nourished, supported, nursed, defended in the face of the Gossiping Chickens is saying NO to me? No to my plant-roots? No to the effort and struggle it took to bring them over from Olde Stable Farm?"

Muriel's quills were standing on end. Indeed, some had already fired off in all directions, causing Cedric to warn, "Quick! Avoid the arrows of outrageous fortune!"

Cedric and Christine sought refuge behind the legs of Cedric's comfy old chair as Muriel shrieked, quills firing willy-nilly, "Is this little frog saying NO to me? Is this the thanks I get for all I've done for you? Am I being rejected?" Quivering in outrage she growled through clenched teeth, "Watch your backs. Strangers in the camp! Strangers, I say!"

Christine did a strange thing. Flying a bit lopsided from her damp wings, she flapped over to Muriel and stroked the back of her ears, saying gently, "We are not rejecting the plant-roots. We are not rejecting you." Continuing to rub behind Muriel's ears, Christine again said, *"We are not rejecting you!"*

Angels are not governed by time or space, and so Christine, although still an angel in training, was able to create *connection* very quickly. As she had with Cedric, so with Muriel she used her power of intuition to create the space of intimacy. What might take weeks or months to establish between animals or Big People, who do not know the spiritual principles or about being in The Process, angels can create in literally seconds. Christine knew how to reach Muriel. She was practicing The Process.

However, the angel also needs the creature's response. The angel cannot make relationship if the other party is not in *soul* agreement. It is possible to reject the message of an angel, and many do. Muriel wanted deep in her soul to be *reached*.

Then Cedric saw the unbelievable. He had to pinch his little knees to know that he was not dreaming. This was stranger than finding an angel in the pond. Muriel began to sob. The iron maiden of Olde Stable Farm, the one who knew all things with the equal assurance of the Rain-God, was actually sobbing! As Christine gently stroked the backs of her ears, soothing the prickly quills, Muriel's whole body shook and throbbed, the sobbing so loud, so heavy, so deep, so *more* — the angel had unleashed the *more*!

The sobbing lasted many minutes. Five, ten, maybe more than twenty minutes. A life-time of pain erupting in almost primal howls. Then silence. Cedric looked at Christine. Her yellow glow-energy warmed the room as she continued to stroke Muriel's ears.

Cedric broke the silence with some nervous frog humour. "I never knew plant-roots meant so much to you!" They immediately burst into laughter. Almost unthinkingly, instinctively, they formed a circle. They were hugging each other. Muriel gazed upon Cedric and Christine with tearful eyes that reflected an inner contentment. All three looked into each other's eyes... and it was comfortable. No awkwardness. No embarrassment. They all glowed.

The Seekers

Later, all three were sitting on Cedric's carpet and Muriel asked Christine in her typical three-peat manner: "You said that I am part of the reason you are here. Did I mishear you? How am I involved in your being here?"

Christine smiled. "I knew when you first bustled into the cottage carrying the precious plant-roots that you were efficient, capable and generous. A special creature. But I also saw that your take-charge energy suffocates your generous spirit, exhausting everyone including yourself. I'm sure many at Olde Stable Farm have grown dependent upon you. But they don't need a caretaker. It has not worked. You need to move from being a caretaker... to being a healer."

Cedric couldn't resist an opportunity to quote a line he had heard often from Mrs. Ramsbottom at the Service of Gratitude. However, he couldn't exactly remember who said it so he confidently ascribed it to a famous character in history:

"Remember what Moses said to Pharoah about 'Physician, heal thyself'. We all need to begin with ourselves."

Muriel rattled her quills at Cedric, annoyed at his interruption. Her interest had been quickened, and she wanted to hear more. "How do I become a healer?"

"You become a healer by first being healed. The process of your healing was started tonight. I was telling Cedric that many of the Big People had become sad and depressed because they had become disconnected from the Spiritual Principles. They are so busy judging each other and telling each other how to live that they create separation.

"The first Principle is Insight. We all, everyone, reflect something of the creator God. The second Principle is Wisdom. To know this stimulates The Process of respecting our differences and learning from them. And the third Principle is Harmony. This is the path to peace."

Genesis flashed into Christine's consciousness. She knew instantly she was sounding like a preacher. She recognized that Muriel's face was becoming more crinkled and perplexed by the minute.

"Let me put it this way," she continued. "In a nutshell..."

"I love nuts," Muriel mused. Indeed, her mind had started to wander.

Christine took a deep breath and continued. "We become healers when we recognize that we are all connected. I understand you because there have been times that I have been in pain and I kept it inside. "

"Angels experience pain?" exclaimed Muriel. "Let me see if I understand you. You are saying that you have sobbed like I just sobbed. You've been that emotional?"

Cedric felt a need to distance Christine from too close a comparison with Muriel. "You mean you felt an angel pain. An angelic sob."

"No," Christine was emphatic. "I mean I've felt pain. Loss. Feeling hop-less. Remember, angels need to grow. They need to evolve. That's how they become healers.

"In a previous life I loved somebody very much. More than I loved myself. I wanted to spend my life, my existence with him... forever. But he did not love me. He loved somebody else. For many years I lived to make him love me, using drama, control, and every manipulation on the planet. But it didn't work. I wasted many years. Today I realize that sometimes you must love somebody enough to let him go. I know what it is to experience the feeling of not being loved in the way you want. I know what it is to be hurt by an unrequited love. Oh yes, I've felt pain.

"I can only be intuitive because I've been where you are. When you see me glow, it's because I've made connection. Our energies intertwine and create a oneness. That is when the spiritual process becomes real. That is The Process.

"The Big People miss this simple truth by establishing religious institutions with rigid rules and national prejudices. These institutions have become holy prisons that separate people from the healing energy, divine intuition, the power to co-create. They separate themselves from The Process and each other."

"I always thought the Big People were crazy," said Cedric. "And now an angel has confirmed it. Oscar Whatshisname hit it on the nose when he said that each man kills the thing he loves."

Christine continued. "The tragedy can be summed up in one sentence: They manipulate the things of God, and in so doing, they disconnect themselves from the spiritual process. If you condemn strangers because they are different, how can you ever celebrate unity?"

Muriel started to feel a little uneasy. The reference to the Big People's concept of strangers seemed all too reminiscent!

Christine glowed brighter as she continued. "The religions of the Big People associate goodness with perfection, and only those who appear perfect are considered to be good, honorable, respectable or...

acceptable. The Big People create so much unhappiness by stuffing their true feelings, hiding who they really are, pretending to be what they are not, and they do all this to be... acceptable."

Cedric and Muriel looked at each other and shaking their heads said in unison, "Gosh, the Big People are in deep dooey!"

Christine smiled at their quick understanding. "Always there are a few Big People who sense what is happening and try to steer others back on track. These are the seekers. They are usually rejected, imprisoned or crucified — but always they touch others and create *connection.* Seekers who in turn create seekers."

Muriel interjected: "Do these seekers have anything in common?"

"Pain," said Christine. "The pain that comes with facing their shadows. In order for the seekers to become the healers they are intended to be, they must go through a re-birthing. The initial cry that accompanies their entry into this life from their previous existence is re-experienced when they seek to move people into The Process. This is what your sobbing was about, Muriel. You were connecting to your pain, and *if you choose*, it can be a re-birthing. You can move into The Process."

Christine suddenly remembered a story Genesis had told her concerning the seeker, Jesus. Jesus had been traveling all day with his disciples when he became aware of a young man following him. The young man asked Jesus how he could become a disciple. Jesus responded, "Read the teachings of the prophets and follow the Torah. Respect your parents and the elders." The young man protested that he already did those things, and pressed Jesus for more. Jesus told him: "Give away all your possessions, then you can be my disciple." The young man walked away with a heavy heart, for he was very wealthy.

Genesis told Christine that Jesus had made many sacrifices to become a seeker. He loved parties, enjoyed good food, was attractive to the ladies and often celebrated his evenings in the taverns with other young men. To be a seeker, he needed to follow a different path. Genesis, who was there during this encounter, knew that Jesus had made connection with the young man. Jesus knew how hard it was for the young man to give up his rich social life. Genesis always believed that a part of Jesus walked away with that young man.

Muriel brought Christine back into the present. "What causes the re-birthing? Meeting an angel? Facing your pain?"

Christine was now glowing bright yellow. It radiated throughout the room so that the singing choirs around Tunbridge Pond were intrigued by the brilliant light blazing from the windows of Cedric's cottage.

"He must be having a party!" exclaimed his all too numerous relatives. Proverbially, Mrs. Ramsbottom, the wise old owl remarked, "Our time will come soon enough."

Both Cedric and Muriel were excited. "Tell us how we get re-birthed!"

"Meeting another seeker. One who has been where you are and is willing to share the journey to the next step. A transforming moment. The touch that allows space for the healing. An intuitive word. A smile that reflects the loving face of God. Yes... meeting another seeker."

A silence fell upon the group. It had been a long day. And now as naturally as the conversation had begun, so sleep followed.

A Conversation With Genesis

Christine only appeared to sleep. She used the time to contact Genesis. She needed some help. This was the first time she was on her own doing angel business!

"How do you think I'm doing?" asked Christine.

"Great," said Genesis in his raspy voice. "Remember you have wisely chosen certain limitations in this adventure, and you're a little like a fallen angel. Ha Ha." Genesis was the only one laughing at his little joke.

Christine wanted reassurance. "Am I making sense? It's quite a leap from Gary Zukav to a frog and a hedgehog."

"Not really," said Genesis. "No offense to Gary. People and animals are basically the same. In fact, you will find that most animals are more naturally inclined to The Process. Their instinct is based upon the Spiritual Principles. Gary Zukav is having a tough time persuading people to accept the idea of non-physical spirit guides. Your problem is that they accept you too readily."

"What do you mean?" asked Christine.

"Well, they expect you to fix them," continued Genesis. "They think you have arrived with all the answers and all they need to do is ask the right questions. Empower them to experience The Process in their own lives. They're going to need it."

"I'm sorry I've limited myself," said Christine. "Can you tell me what to expect?"

"I can, but I won't," said Genesis. "Use the same principles you expect them to use. It will help you with your own evolvement. After all, even with all your angel powers you don't know everything. Neither do I. Become an angelic mirror to who they are. That's the adventure. I think you're going to love it."

"Do they know their negativity and pain brought me to them?" she asked.

Genesis pulled his earring impatiently. "Please, Christine. Get with The Process. They've only just met you. They suspect that there must be a reason for your being here, but not enough has happened yet for them to put it together. Come to think of it, you've not put it together yourself."

Christine changed the subject. "Why did you put that Jesus story in my mind? Was it a subtle hint?"

Genesis grimaced in frustration, pulling on his earring. "The things that bring us to The Process are often the hardest to let go. You'll discover this when the time comes to leave your new friends. I'll miss Gary when my time comes to move on. Attachments, more than anything, hinder The Process. I'm beginning to understand that our spiritual goal is detachment. This is not to be confused with disconnection. But that's for another story."

"You mean I'm not going to come back here?" queried Christine.

Genesis looked intently at her. "Remember what we've both learned together. Connection never ends. A part of you will be forever here at Tunbridge Pond. Now go back to your new friends... and don't preach." With that, Genesis was gone, leaving a trace of spice in the air.

Intimacy

It was late in the morning and Cedric, Muriel and Christine were still sleeping on the carpet. Their sleep was disturbed by a banging at the cottage door.

"Hello. Is anybody here? Hello." It was the voice of Roger the Fox. He had been listening to the early morning gossip and had heard about the mysterious stranger. Christine had been described as the "glow-creature" and more than one informant had made the observation that *she* was pretty. That was enough for Roger. A possible new conquest he could not refuse.

"Hello. Cedric. It's me. Roger. Hello!"

"Coming. I'm coming, Roger. Wait!" Cedric opened the door and before he could say "come in" Roger was into the room.

"Well, hello," said Roger as he moved towards Christine. "I see you have a guest, my dear Cedric. How nice."

Muriel called out, "Hello, Roger. I'm over here. Your favorite little hedgehog is smiling at you!" Muriel always needed to remind people that she was special to them.

Roger smiled at both the greeters but his eyes were firmly fixed upon Christine. "Well, my dear. And who might you be?" Roger had moved very near to Christine and had positioned himself so that he was looking down at her as she fluttered maybe a foot off the ground. Her wings had completely dried during the night and she enjoyed hovering. This is the normal position for angels when they are not traveling.

"My name is Christine. I'm an angel."

"You certainly are! There is no denying that fact... yes... my name is Roger. As you can see, I'm a fox. I'm also single... yes... how nice to meet you. I don't think I've ever met an angel before... yes... what lovely hair. What a lovely shape — I mean — body. What beautiful eyes. Yes indeed, you certainly bring a glow to this cottage! Don't you agree, Cedric? Of course you do."

Roger moved around the room and gave a friendly sniff to Muriel and Cedric but always his eyes were on Christine.

"Will you be staying long? Have you had lunch? I'm single you know. There is a delightful place where we could find some fresh partridge eggs. Do you like eggs for breakfast? Do angels eat? I suppose you must eat something to get the energy to flap those beautiful wings."

"I receive my energy from the environment. Everything in the forest, everything around the pond... everything in this room gives me energy."

Roger only appeared to listen. His lecherous mind was working overtime. He was alone with Christine in the forest, they'd finished the eggs and he was about to lick her little angel neck.

Roger smacked his lips as he imagined Christine's seduction. He had not gone far in his lascivious daydream when Christine faltered. Within seconds, she dropped to the carpet.

"Are you okay?" asked Cedric.

"Can I get you some plant-roots?" asked Muriel. She was hungry and hated to eat alone. She rarely prepared a meal for herself. "Can I fix us all some plant-roots?"

Roger leered at Christine. "I seem to have this effect on the opposite sex."

Muriel bristled her quills, muttering under her breath, "Watch your backs. Strangers in the camp. Strangers, I say!"

Ignoring her, Roger continued, "Really... they go faint in my presence."

"Why do you want to lick my neck?" Christine asked.

Roger's jaw dropped. Speechless, he gawked at Christine as the others stared in dumbstruck silence. Roger's tongue returned to his mouth and he swallowed... hard. In the ensuing silence, Cedric and Muriel looked at Roger expectantly.

"Why do you want to lick my neck?" Christine repeated her question.

Roger began to splutter. "What are you talking about? Lick whose neck? Really. This must be angel humour. Ha Ha. Ha... Ha... Well, I don't exactly want to lick your neck. Gosh, this is embarrassing... it's more like affection. That's all it is. Affection."

Christine looked intently at Roger and said, "Tell me if I've got it right so far. We've eaten the eggs. Actually, you ate the eggs, Roger. We sit on the rock. You suggest I look at the beautiful clouds and then, as I look at the sky, you gaze at my neck and... you want to lick it."

"Oh, my God. Have we met before? Are you Jasmine, or possibly Penelope, or maybe Gertrude — have you taken on another form and returned to haunt me? Have we done breakfast before? Oh, dear, I've been with so many it's hard to remember."

"No, Roger. I've never met you before but of course, I've met many creatures like you."

Cedric shook his head and smiled. He knew Roger had met his match.

"Roger, this is Christine. Remember, and please hear me this time — she's an *angel*. Christine, this is Roger."

Muriel interrupted. "I'm sure I'm not the only one who's hungry. Golly gosh, it's time to eat. We all need some food in our bellies."

"Thank you, Muriel. I don't know what we'd do without you," said Roger.

"You'd learn to take care of yourselves." Christine could not resist a little dig.

"What made you lose your balance a bit ago? Were you feeling sick?" Cedric asked Christine.

"Not really. I'll explain in a moment. First let me say hello to Roger. I'm sorry if I startled you with sharing aloud what you were thinking, but I was a little startled, too. Also, I think it was good I interrupted you before you got carried away. Don't you agree, Roger?"

It's hard to see if a fox is embarrassed but behind the red fur was bright pink skin! "Yes... if you put it like that... I certainly agree," said Roger.

Christine continued. "Angels connect. Always remember that simple fact. The nature of angels is to be *at one* with their surroundings and so when you entered the cottage I connected with you. Remember that good thoughts, positive energy, happiness and joy, healthy struggle and honest conversation makes me glow... like a light. I receive energy from everything in the room and if the energy is spiritual, then I glow. By the way, so do you. Connection ignites a light that shines in the darkness.

"But when I am being used, when my identity is not respected or cherished, when I become an object for another's pleasure, or when the spiritual connection is being rejected, then I grow dim, my energy drains and I begin to falter... maybe even fall. That's what happened a few minutes ago.

"Roger, in your mind you were using me, taking from me without my consent. I was the object of your desires. A sexual object. But you had no regard for my feelings. You were not wanting connection. It was all about what you wanted. That drained my energy and I fell to the carpet."

Roger exclaimed as he chewed on the plant-roots, "My dear, you're better than Mrs. Ramsbottom. Don't tell her I said that. You size a person up in a minute. You are so intuitive. So perceptive. I wish I could be like you."

"You can, Roger. You already are. Think about what you do when you first meet a creature of the opposite sex. You use your intuition to strike up a conversation. You are perceptive about what your chances are of scoring — adding another conquest to your collection."

Muriel began to splutter and cough. She was a little embarrassed at hearing the words scoring and conquest coming from an angel, so early in the morning.

Then Christine said something that got everybody's attention. "Oh yes, Roger, you are a seeker who is going down the wrong path."

Muriel thought to herself, "Roger, a seeker?" Cedric looked equally surprised. Christine turned and smiled at them both.

"Yes, Roger is a seeker. But at the moment, you are painfully hunting for prey instead of developing I-N-T-I-M-A-C-Y. What you want is intimacy. What you create is your own *loneliness*. Sex is no substitute for intimacy."

"Easier said than done," said Roger. They all chuckled.

Another silence followed as everyone chewed on the plant-roots. There was a contentment around the table — although not a glow. Muriel shuffled uneasily and then spoke.

"Roger, you are not alone in learning something about yourself from Christine. I learned something last night. She told me that I was accepted... that I was good enough. I literally fell apart hearing it. But it wasn't just the words that created the eruption of feeling. You see, Christine touched me. She stroked the back of my ears like my mother used to do before... before... " Muriel was holding back her tears when she said, "...before my mother left me and my three brothers. Good gracious. I pray to the Rain-God that I can tell this without crying again... Before my mother left us she would always spend time rubbing the back of our ears saying how much she loved us. Then Hector from the next village came and asked her to join him in the new nest he was building. She said she loved us, but she left us for Hector.

"I was the oldest, so I had to take over. It was really hard. I knew they all depended on me, and I was so scared. I wasn't grown yet either, and Mother hadn't taught me how to teach young ones what they need to know. I would lie awake at night worrying if I was leaving something important out. And I always thought Mother would come back, and I wanted her to be proud of me. I was afraid if I wasn't good enough, she'd go away again. You know, I've never really put it into words before, but all my life I've never felt good enough... in myself. Never felt... "

Christine remembered her unrequited love. The love that had not been returned in the way she had wanted. An unnoticed tear fell from her eye. She still loved him.

An idea popped into Cedric's mind: could this be what Christine called insight — learning things about ourselves? Excited to share his new thought, he interrupted. "This reminds me of the ugly duckling story — you know, the one about the swan who thought she was ugly because she didn't know she was a swan —"

"Just listen, Cedric. Just listen. Muriel is becoming a healer," whispered Christine. "See how she is glowing?"

Muriel indeed glowed brighter as she continued. "I had to keep it a secret that I really didn't know how to teach the young ones. So I got in the habit of just doing it for them. I guess I thought then they'd know what to do. I think... I think that's when I started getting so bossy. If things were done properly, then it meant I was doing a good job." Muriel paused for a moment, struggling to put words to the recognition dawning within her.

"How did you know you were doing a good job?" Christine asked.

"Well, I guess... I didn't, not really, unless friends told me."

"How did they tell you? How do you know?" Christine gently guided her.

"Well... if they tell me I'm special, and seem to want me to be around all the time..." Muriel began to glow brighter, alight with insight. "That's it! That's why I'm so bossy, and why I'm always taking care of other people. I fear if I don't hold on to you, chain you down, make you appreciate all I do for you — that I will fail and you will leave me. Like Mother.

Christine's touch reminded me of my mother, and all that I lost when she left.

"So I had to be more perfect, more precise, more definite, more capable more... more... more... RIGHT. All my life I took care of my brothers and still do. I take care of the animals at Olde Stable Farm. I tried to take care of Cedric, everybody... and now I see that it didn't, hasn't, will not work... I need to heal. I need to change... I need to... relax."

Muriel turned to look at Christine. "I don't know what you did when you touched me, but I am different. Something inside me wants to come out. I feel... I feel a glow."

"And we can see it," Cedric smiled.

"Yes, I am feeling it with you," said Christine.

Cedric looked at Roger. To his surprise, Roger was not glowing. He looked attentive; he'd certainly been taking it all in, but he was grinning nervously. Instead of a glow, he exuded anxious energy. Feeling Cedric's sudden agitation, Christine and Muriel both turned to look at Roger.

"Uh. I'm beginning to feel a slight tingle inside me," said Roger. "I could see Muriel was onto something. I found myself cheering her on inside — wanting her to get it. I mean — for her to find her process. I was shouting inside for her. And now I know that I was not shouting to Muriel alone, I was shouting to myself." Roger looked at the three faces staring expectantly at him. He realized with a start that they were waiting for him to tell them why he was shouting for himself. Trying to get himself off the hook, he'd just put his neck in the noose!

He was aware of his own secret feelings coming to the surface as he listened to Muriel. But he had no intention of letting outsiders know of the deep pain he carried inside. Over the years, Roger had perfected the art of eliciting sympathy without really being vulnerable. Not deep down where it counted. He was a tricky performer, appearing to be open and sympathetic, but always holding back the real truth of his hurts at the hands of Ramsay the Wolf. With years of practice, he had gotten the story down pat. It was part of his seduction routine — slyly seducing others into thinking he was revealing his innermost self.

Mistaking his silence for shyness, Muriel encouraged Roger. "Why were you shouting for yourself, Roger? *You* never have a problem with self-confidence!"

He took a deep breath, thinking, "OK. It's showtime!" He licked his lips nervously, fumbling for words. "Uh, no. Not with that, but... Trust. I have a problem with trust. All my life, I seem to look at life from the outside. Like watching a drama that somehow involves me, but I'm never sure quite how."

Cedric almost blurted out, "Like Hamlet — " but stopped himself in time. He sensed that this was not a time for a wise quote.

"I don't think I ever got over the suicide of my brother. Our mother was killed by hunters when we were three months old. I — I guess that makes us alike, huh Muriel." He ducked his head shyly in her direction. "But I didn't have a big sister to take care of me. A big old wolf named Ramsay took us in and raised us as his own. He tried to make a family, but it... wasn't the same.

"You see, when my mother was killed, my brother, he... thought it was all his fault. Mother knew the hunters were in the area, and was trying to get us back to the den. But Reggie — he stopped to play with some bugs. He was having so much fun he didn't realize Mother meant business trying to hurry him along. The hunters heard him and shot Mother. She barely got us back to the den before she died."

"Reggie was never the same. He never played anymore, and hardly would leave the den. He just knew it was all his fault. And when things got bad with Ramsay, he blamed himself for that, too. One evening, before his first birthday, he threw himself off Barton Tower Bridge. And something within me died with him."

Roger sneaked a sideways glance at his audience. Muriel and Cedric were looking at him sorrowfully, tears of sympathy trickling down Muriel's cheeks. "Gotcha!" he snickered to himself. Those two were such pushovers. But he could not read Christine. She looked just as sympathetic, but still, he wasn't sure she was buying it. Time to pour on the fox-craft.

"Christine, I know that you can help me. I know there is a lot more that needs to be said about my brother's suicide. It has been a heavy burden to carry. I felt I should have done more to help him, to protect him. I spent too much time away and not enough time with my brother. I didn't know how badly Ramsay was... hurting him. I mean, he... hurt us both, but I thought — I thought I'd taken most of it."

Like all good liars, Roger knew the secret was in telling part of the truth; the manipulation and dishonesty lay then in what he did *not* say. Which was that he had become a willing participant in Ramsay's wicked ways. All of his seductiveness, his trickery and cunning, he had learned from Ramsay. Not only learned it, but perfected it. Became it. And had used it on Reggie. Although he tried to convince himself that most everyone was naive and gullible, secretly, he believed others were pulling the same kind of charade on him. So, in truth, he did not trust. Because he did not trust, he often tried to beat others at their own game, putting on a charade that masked his real feelings.

"Christine, I believe you can help me. What can I do about the guilt I feel for my brother's suicide. The shame of my own abuse. The self-loathing that I carry covering my behavior. Tell me what I must do."

Instinctively, Muriel moved and rubbed the side of her head against Roger's front paws. Cedric also moved closer. Christine fluttered her wings so that she was above all three. She still glowed, but noticeably dimmer. Although she appeared to be looking at all of them, Roger sensed she was really looking at him, seeing his charade, and he hated that -- hated Christine for seeing through him.

Roger hated feeling so vulnerable. He had said too much to the little group. Normally, he did not feel guilt when he told lies in order to seduce others for his own gain. Now he was feeling strangely guilty. It made him feel sick to his stomach. He was angry. He sensed he had not tricked Christine, and she might tell Cedric and Muriel. Roger wanted revenge. A part of him wanted to rip into all of them and kill them and nobody would be the wiser. Better not. He would wait. And he knew he would have his revenge. As he listened to them chattering away, he knew things would never be the same. Revenge. So he asked again, seeming so sad about it, "Tell me what I must do."

"Let me pray about it." said Christine.

"Do angels pray? Do angels need to pray? I thought you knew everything," said Muriel in amazement.

" William Snakespit says that prayer is the song of angels," said Cedric.

Christine smiled at Cedric. "Prayer for me is connection. Sometimes I just need to rest in the presence of THE ONE WHO KNOWS. It's not about what I say. It's about absorbing the energy. I need to be uncluttered. Only then will the Spiritual Principles of Insight, Wisdom and Harmony become real."

Christine then turned and faced Muriel. "It's not that I need to pray. I *am* the prayer. I want to feel the energy from THE ONE WHO KNOWS. You call him the Rain-God. The prayer is connection. Gratitude."

"Then you will enjoy our Service of Gratitude. Everyone will be there," said Muriel.

"First, I go to pray." said Christine.

Muriel continued, "You pray. We'll eat the plant-roots. Before they get cold."

While the three of them laughed at her clever remark, Christine flew to the window and stared out at the Sun. In the light of the window she reflected a translucent beauty that was almost formless. Cedric, Muriel and Roger knew she was there but you had to look really hard to see her. *If you were not looking for an angel, you would not see one.*

"I'm really enjoying Christine," said Muriel. "How long will she stay?"

Roger, speaking in a wily tone that usually indicated trickery, interjected, "I'm sure she will not stay too long. Angels have better things to do than hang around Olde Stable Farm and Tunbridge Pond. There is nothing really for her to do. Our problems pale in comparison to the craziness of the Big People. We'll just have to be content with getting our spiritual lessons from Mrs. Ramsbottom."

"I don't know how long she will stay, " said Cedric. "I'll ask her when she returns. Yes, it would be wonderful to have her around but... somehow... I don't think she will stay. I know one thing, when she does go, I'm going to miss her. I can't believe that she has only been with me one day. So much has happened. So many incredible things have happened in such a short time.

"To think I started out yesterday full of gloom and despondency. I was in a toad mood." Frogs used this remark to convey misery. It was an ancient expression that revealed the on-going prejudice that existed between toads and frogs. Toads were always the butt of frog jokes — and toads had similar feelings about frogs. In this way, they established a necessary difference: frogs were not toads!

Cedric continued, "I was in a toad of a mood. I didn't know what was wrong but I felt really sad. The pits. I'd even contemplated taking the Big Splash!"

"Oh, no. Don't say that. Please don't even say such a thing!" cried Muriel.

"Remember, I know what the Big Splash does to those who are left to go on. It creates a horrible pain," said Roger.

"Okay, I know you both are right. But what I'm trying to tell you is that yesterday was a horrid day. And within hours everything — I mean everything — was different. At this moment, I feel an energy that I have never felt in my life before. Christine has brought a glow. I feel it. I don't mean to be sacriligious, but after I've spent hours praying to the Rain-God, and I didn't think that anything could bring more power than praying to the Rain-God, even that never made me feel this way.

"So much has come from that little plop — that little 'Help me! Help me!' Christine was the one who cried for help, but I'm the one who was rescued," sighed Cedric.

"I know exactly what you mean," said Muriel.

"We all know exactly what you mean," said Roger.

Muriel continued, "It's like we needed her. We drew her into our lives."

"She'd been visiting a Big Person named Gary Zukav and she was returning home... to Paradise. And then she miscalculated her distance from the surface of the water and fell in. That's what she said," mused Cedric.

"Well, she certainly creates an impression. I've met some chicks in my time, but she's got a quiet style. You're never quite sure what she's thinking," said Roger.

"Not unlike you, Roger," said Cedric perceptively. He was beginning to use the Spiritual Principle of Insight.

"I've never been so honest in my life. I'm embarrassed to think about it. And all those tears. That heavy sobbing. I sobbed myself right back to my childhood," said Muriel.

"I wonder how she knew to touch my ears. The feel of her touch felt exactly like... Mother's." Tears were again developing in Muriel's eyes. "How could she know that?"

Another silence fell upon the group and then Cedric jerked his head up. He looked startled. "Maybe you told her. Yes... that's it. You told her, Muriel. Remember what she said. We give her energy. She knows what we are thinking... Remember when Roger was... thinking about Christine —- " Cedric was getting excited now. "We give her not just words and thoughts but memories. She feels, she sees, she experiences what we are feeling, seeing, experiencing. The pain of your mother had not left you. It was still in your memory banks, Muriel. She saw what you were remembering."

"Yes," said Muriel. "She said something about that earlier. Do you remember, she said that she connects with our energy. She is only reflecting back to us what we give her."

"That was certainly true for me," said Roger. He was beginning to feel a little uneasy. He wondered if she knew he was holding back. Had she picked up on his secret?

Cedric smiled. His brown-green-yellow skin really glowed. His eyes were bright and clear. He exuded excited energy.

"*We* drew Christine to us. We were screaming for her and... yes, now I understand... she plopped into the pond.

"Remember she said that when she is around negative energy, the energy that uses and abuses, she feels drained... suffocated... the opposite of the glow. She was flying over Olde Stable Farm and Tunbridge Pond and she was affected by *our* pain, *our* sadness... "

"Oh, my Rain-God. This is scary. She may know more than we think," Roger said anxiously. He was more determined than ever to cover the traces of his apparent vulnerability. His large tongue licked his lips as he tasted the sweetness of his revenge.

"She is here," said Cedric, "because she has something to do. Maybe she has a message for all of us."

"Even Mrs. Ramsbottom?" laughed Muriel.

Cedric was serious. "Yes, even Mrs. Ramsbottom. This is no mistake!"

"What's that shining in my eyes?" cried Cedric.

"It's me," said Christine. "You are filling me with joy, with love, with wisdom. I can hardly contain the glow that is within me. Roger, are you listening? It's better than sex!"

Roger looked embarrassed and pushed his nose under the table. Everyone, began to laugh. Roger elicited a sly grin.

"But you are so right," said Christine. "You *called* me here. I have something to do. And it's not so unlike what Genesis is doing with Gary Zukav and the seekers. I feel as if I'm in familiar territory. The challenges are the same. The pain looks the same. However, you are much quicker than the Big People. Your vulnerability is so much closer to the surface that the *connection* comes that much quicker. Truly. It would take twenty years for some Big People to get this. Poor Genesis is exhausted. And some Big People never get it."

"They sound like toads," joked Cedric.

"Much worse," said Christine.

"Really? Wow!" Cedric exclaimed.

"How long will you stay with us?" asked Muriel.

"As long as it takes. I'd like to visit Olde Stable Farm later this afternoon. Then I will be more clear."

"Tonight we have a Service of Gratitude to the Rain-God, followed by a community meeting. Something has been brewing for weeks with Betty, Alice and Irma and I wouldn't be surprised if it didn't erupt in your presence. Let's face it, Christine. Everything seems to happen when you are around."

"Is that a compliment? Thank you!" said Christine.

"You make life... how can I say this... you make life *more life*," said Muriel.

"That word *more* word keeps coming up. I really like it because it is so expansive. But some day you must discover what the more looks like," said Christine.

"You bring us all together. You..." Muriel felt the need to praise Christine.

"Please," said Christine. "Don't miss your part in all of this. We all, together, help create the *more*. Remember what I have been saying. The More is in The Process. It is making the Spiritual Principles of Insight, Wisdom and Harmony come alive in ordinary situations. Genesis is forever telling me that the job of an angel is to reflect back to you the moves *you* are already making. Transformation can never be achieved if you believe that somebody else is doing it for you. Think of me more like a coach than a magician. This is why I am here."

"Won't THE ONE WHO KNOWS and the other angels in Paradise miss you?"

"Oh, no. I will be here for as long as it takes and then I will continue with my journey. Remember, with angels there is no time. Only the experience. Paradise is timeless. The Past is rolled into the Future and the Future is happening now. Once we have connected, I can never really leave you. *I am with you always*. That is a quote from Jesus the Seeker."

"All the Big People seem to quote this Jesus character. Was he very special?" asked Cedric.

"Oh, yes. He *is* special. At certain times when the need on earth is great, The Process becomes flesh, usually a Big Person who comes with a message. Most of the Big People don't understand. They aren't able to make *connection*. They are so busy defending their rules, protecting their religious dogmas, guarding their spiritual purity, that they miss completely the gift that is before them. The Process is calling out to them from every rock, tree, creature and sunset. They refuse to hear it or see it. I'll say it again — *connect*. One such time lasted thirty-three years, and the messenger's name was Jesus. Many believe he was really THE ONE WHO KNOWS in human form.

"The Big People rejected him. Well, that's not completely true. Always there are the seekers. They come alive when they are connected with The Process. Though they are few in number, they are found within all the religions... and none.

"The Process is also alive in some creatures. I believe it is alive in you. I know it is. The energy of THE ONE WHO KNOWS is active in all creation. The gift of Insight allows us to recognize it. All creation radiates this powerful energy and comes together to produce Harmony."

Christine grabbed some plant-roots from Muriel. "Make connection with the food we eat, and so often take for granted. Smell it. Feel it. Appreciate it. The food we eat, the trees, streams, rocks — all of our world is part of The Process. The seekers intuitively understand that everything is involved in The Process."

Cedric could not resist singing a song he had heard on the Big People's radio:

"*I see trees of green, I watch them grow. And I said to myself* —" Muriel and Roger joined in for the dramatic finale, "*What a wonderful world*."

They then burst into laughter. Christine continued, finishing her point. "Genesis tells me that more and more Big People, as they become increasingly disillusioned with institutional religion, are becoming seekers. Their numbers are growing. The Big People are seeking what most animals instinctively have."

Cedric remembered something else he had read: "And a lamb shall lead them." He thought, why not a frog?

Visiting Olde Stable Farm

Now it was time to begin the journey to Olde Stable Farm. Cedric, Muriel and Roger were really excited about Christine meeting with all the other animals. They were both proud and excited. *They* had an angel for a friend. They were also pleased to be the chosen ones to make the introduction!

Christine knew what they were thinking and she smiled within herself. Genesis had told her that people tended to place angels on pedestals and this needed to change before there could ever be a *real connection*. Genesis had not said anything about animals! But Christine knew that if she worked on the relationship becoming real, ego and grandstanding would eventually give way to *connection*.

"I wonder how the animals will take to Christine?" asked Roger.

"She'll handle them. Christine knows how to handle everything. Just watch her," replied Muriel.

"It will be what it is meant to be" Cedric reflected. He was pleasantly surprised at his developing wisdom. He was beginning to sound like Christine.

What a funny sight they must have appeared to any onlookers as they walked along Stable Road. A hopping frog, a shuffling hedgehog, a prancing fox and a hovering angel. Not an everyday sight, you must agree. It was a two-mile walk from the cottage to Olde Stable Farm. As they talked and enjoyed the company of each other, it seemed to take no time at all. Funny how when you are really enjoying yourself time seems to disappear. Perhaps that's how Paradise became timeless.

As they entered the gates that marked the entrance to Olde Stable Farm they were greeted by the gossiping trio: Alice, Betty and Irma. They spoke all at once, and it was difficult to know who was saying what. "Hello, hello, hello. Cedric, we are surprised to see you. We thought you might miss the Service of Gratitude this evening, too busy entertaining your new friend. I expect she's an old friend. I expect she's an old friend from the past. We understand she stayed the night with you! My, my. How friendly, and how happy you all seem. Quite the little family!"

They continued clucking in a rapid chatter. "Hello, Muriel. Hello Roger. My my. Yes you are quite the little family."

Toby the sheepdog bounded into the group, frightening the chickens, sniffing Muriel and licking his friend Roger, and accidentally squashing little Cedric under his paws.

"Get off me! Get off! You four-legged catastrophe. Get off me!" cried Cedric.

"I'm sorry. I'm so sorry. I'm just so pleased to see you. Everybody says you have a new friend. Has she gone home? Where is she?"

"I'm here," said Christine. She was so small it was easy to miss her, especially if you were a peripatetic sheepdog called Toby! Cedric dusted himself down, straightened himself up and announced to the attending group. "Listen everyone. This is Christine. She is... wait for it... she is an A-N-G-E-L!"

"You've been been dating dating dating an angel angel angel?" shrieked Alice, Betty and Irma in the closest approximation of unison they had managed in years.

"I've not been dating anyone. Christine is my new friend. We met along the way and she will stay until she departs!" proclaimed Cedric.

Everyone looked at one another, silently confused.

"I'm pleased to meet you," Toby said excitedly, breaking the silence. Toby did everything excitedly.

"It's a pleasure, pleasure, pleasure, we're sure, sure, sure!" shrieked Alice, Betty and Irma.

At that moment, Old John, the mule, trotted into the group. All the animals liked John. He was given a similar respect to that afforded Mrs. Ramsbottom, but he nevertheless carried what everybody agreed was a heavy heart.

John could be pig-headed. Betsy, the pig, hated this term because it labeled all pigs as stubborn or unyielding. She felt it was unfair to all pigs, not least herself. She had never met a pig who was stubborn or unyielding, except when they were being taken to become Sunday lunch for the Big People. In these circumstances, what animal wouldn't be unyielding! Betsy felt that pigs were getting a bad reputation with this term and so nobody used the P-H word in Betsy's company. However, away from Betsy's hearing, when the animals talked about John, he was described as pig-headed and mighty stubborn.

He had been around Olde Stable Farm for twenty years or more and nobody understood the behaviour of the Big People better than Old John. Rumour had it that he had been in love with a beautiful young mule called Elizabeth. Something happened. She left him. He left her. She got involved with another. He couldn't bring himself to profess his love. Others had heard that he was growing senile. Whatever the cause, Old John was not a happy camper.

John spoke directly to Christine. "I'm John. People called me Old John because I'm old. Pleased to meet you. I heard you're an angel. You bring a blessing to Olde Stable Farm, no doubt about that. We're glad you're here."

"Thank you, John. I don't think you are old. May I just call you John?" said Christine.

"Well... er... yes. That would be fine." John seemed pleased.

They all set off to Jacob's Hill where the service was to be held. All the animals enjoyed the peace and tranquility of Jacob's Hill. For them, it was the special home of the Rain-God. This is where the animals connected to the energy of The Process Christine had talked about. The dewy grass, gentle winds and calming silence that was always present helped to bring a feeling of peace and togetherness to all the animals.

Jacob's Hill was hidden behind the stables and trees that lay to the east of Olde Stable Farm. At the time of the service the Big People had retired to the farmhouse as they always did at about the same time every evening. The animals knew they could meet without fear of being disturbed. The service was always the Service of Gratitude. Big People thought they were

the only creatures who worshipped, but Big People are
ignorant of many things.

Timothy

"H-Hello. H-Hello, suh-Cedric. H-Hi M-Muriel," Timothy stuttered. Timothy liked to consider himself Cedric's best friend but he would never say such a thing. He didn't say very much at all — he was painfully shy. Being a snail who also stuttered didn't help! He was also slow. Painfully slow. He never made any meetings or parties — although he waited to greet all the animals as they started out or were returning from where *he* was meant to be. He usually started out hours before the others and even then he never made it! His nick-name was 'Hello-Goodnight,' because he said hello as they started off and goodnight as they were returning.

"Hello, Hello-Goodnight," said Cedric. "I want you to meet a new friend who is very special. Stay where you are and *don't move*," said Cedric. This was a funny thing to say considering the incredible slowness of Timothy, but Cedric had missed his own joke because he was so excited about Christine meeting Timothy. "Christine, Christine! Please fly over here and meet a friend. We call him Hello-Goodnight but his real name is Timothy."

"I'm very pleased to meet you. I'm an angel and I feel I already know you. You don't have to explain why everybody calls you Hello-Goodnight because I understand. Angels understand many things that are not said. Are you coming to the meeting?"

"Oh, y-yes. I'm c-coming. Buh-but I don't think that I'll arrive. I've been c-coming to every meeting buh-but I never arrive. I think that is part of the reason that I am sh-shy. I never really get to know anyone. Except suh-Cedric. He took time to sit with me. He's the only animal who seems to have the p-patience to sit and talk with me. Also he doesn't interrupt me when I'm trying to say something. He's my sp-special friend."

"I'd also like to be your special friend," said Christine.

"Th-That would be nice. Then I'd have t-two sp-special friends," said Timothy.

"I think I can get you to come to this meeting. Why don't you let me fly you," said Christine. "I promise I won't drop you. Angels are very strong. We are small because we choose to be. And if I choose to have the strength to carry you, I can do so. The energy that surrounds all of us is truly immense. We need only tap into it."

Christine was just about to launch into one of her lectures — really, they were more like mini-sermons unless she checked herself — when a whiff of incense announced Genesis. He rasped into her ear: "Give it a rest." Christine swallowed and smiled at Timothy.

"So I'll just tap into it and — away we'll go!" Christine laughed.

"W-wow! Would you really duh-do that for me? Then I could not only go to a meeting, I could actually arrive!" said Timothy.

"Let's do it," said Christine. She hovered for a moment over Timothy's shell and then she gently mounted him as if she was mounting a race-horse. In a flash he was hovering two or three feet above the ground and heading in the direction of Jacob's Hill. The connection of their bodies created a bright yellow glow that Cedric, Muriel and Roger had seen earlier in the cottage.

When all the animals that had gathered for the Service of Gratitude saw the arrival of Hello-Goodnight, they began to cheer. Mrs. Ramsbottom, who had heard about Cedric's angel friend, was heard to remark, "My word! When Hello-Goodnight finally does arrive, he certainly arrives in style. Few of us arrive at the Service of Gratitude flown in by an angel!"

The Service

Everybody had gathered for the Service of Gratitude. They formed a circle, and Mrs. Ramsbottom stood in the center. There were more than a hundred animals in attendance, yet the Big People were completely unaware. The animals had no fixed places, but some creatures were always together.

This was especially true of Chandu and Chico. These two male Burmese cats lived for each other. They licked each other before and during the service. They were often hugging and rubbing each other. It was definitely love.

Alice, Betty and Irma sat on the opposite side to Chandu and Chico. They never wanted to get too close to the cats. This had nothing to do with the fact that they were cats. It was because they did not approve of the cats' life-style. They had been against Chandu and

Chico from their earliest days. They said their behaviour was foreign, part of their strange oriental religion. Males should not kiss other males. And they were determined to do something about it!

Cedric, Muriel and Toby always sat with Chandu and Chico because they enjoyed them so much. They were fun, affectionate and comfortable to be with. Of course, they knew that their relationship was strange to many animals who lived around Olde Stable Farm, but they appreciated the difference. Chandu and Chico were never offensive, indeed, they were probably the most gentle and loving creatures on the farm. Nobody was too much trouble for them and they went out of their way to be helpful to any creature that needed them. They knew that the chickens and some of the other animals were against the nature of their relationship, but Chandu and Chico never allowed feelings of animosity to affect their loving disposition.

At the Service of Gratitude, Cedric, Muriel and Toby were also joined by Roger, Christine and Timothy. Old John, who usually sat with the stable animals, did an unusual thing at this Service of Gratitude. He made a point of sitting beside Chandu and Chico. It was apparent to everyone that Old John was sending a message with his gesture. He was approving the presence of the two cats. Chico leaned over and greeted him.

The tranquillity of Jacob's Hill grew as the animals quietly took their places. After a moment of silence, as the sun was beginning its descent into Tunbridge Pond, the various birds began their chorus of praise.

"Love and Gratitude we raise
As we join in thankful praise
To the Eternal One."

This chorus of praise was sung repeatedly and all the animals slowly began to join in. Soon everyone had joined with the birds in this powerful song of celebration.

When it was over, Mrs. Ramsbottom lifted her wings. "Peace be to all of you!"

They responded, "May this peace continue to grow."

Christine hovered close to the ground so that she could be near to Timothy. She glowed in appreciation for the simplicity of the worship.

Mrs. Ramsbottom continued. "We meet to celebrate the Rain-God and all other Gods who reflect Peace and Harmony. We seek to honor each creature that lives and moves upon the earth. We accept our responsibility for creating life and love at Olde Stable Farm."

All the animals responded, "In Gratitude we claim our heritage."

Christine could feel their connection vibrating in the ensuing hush. She noticed how unhurried and relaxed everybody seemed. It was truly awesome for her to be in the presence of over one hundred animals who were completely silent.

Old John moved into the circle and began to sing, in a deep and soulful voice, the following refrain.

Hear the silence growing, in each and every heart.
See the love-glow growing, never to depart.
We are one together, knowing we are free.
Let it be. Let it be.

Christine was so excited when she heard John sing. The Process. The glow. The Insight, Wisdom and Harmony. They were all there. The *more* was present in this service.

Out of nowhere a raspy voice spoke to her. "Relax. Enjoy. See what these furry angels have created... out of the mouth of..."

Old John usually gave the animals a tune for them to hang their gratitude upon. He had a knack for composing tunes that had verses everyone could sing together, and then come forward to make up their own personal verses of gratitude. It had become their favorite way of singing together.

Chandu planted a kiss upon the top of Chico's head and moved into the circle. He had a purry voice that was deep and sexy. Even the animals who criticized his behaviour loved to hear him sing.

Hear the silence growing, in each and every heart.

See the love-glow growing, never to depart.
I'm joined here with my only love, knowing we are free.
Let it be. Let it be.

For more than an hour the animals creatively sang their gratitude. Then Roger, who rarely attended the Service of Gratitude, moved into the center. He sang in a foxy snarl, avoiding eye contact with the others.

Hear the silence growing, in each and every heart.
See the love-glow growing, never to depart.
Today I do what I must do, wanting to be free.
Let it be. Let it be.

Next, Muriel bustled into the center of the circle. She sat upright on her hind legs, with her quills fanning out in all directions. She had the presence of an opera diva about to embark on her favourite aria. Her voice was squeaky and clipped, but it resonated all over Jacob's Hill.

When it came to create her special affirmation line, Muriel sang loudly, "Today I know I'm good enough, knowing I am free."

Other animals joined in this Song of Gratitude and the birds kept the melody humming in the back ground.

Timothy, who had never sung before because he'd never arrived, asked Christine if it would be okay for him to sing.

"Of course. They would all love to hear you sing," whispered Christine.

"Buh-but my stutter. I'm afraid my st-stutter will make them laugh," said Timothy.

"Take your strength from the circle of love. Look, I'll move into the center with you."

"You will? You promise?" said Timothy.

"I promise," said Christine.

Alice, Betty and Irma, who always sang as a group, were finishing their chorus. They often came across as a humourous interlude because, although they insisted on singing as a threesome, they all seemed to be singing something different. However, nothing they did could destroy the peace and tranquility of Jacob's Hill.

Timothy began to move to the center, gently pushed by Christine. When the animals saw it was Timothy, a supportive hush descended upon the circle. Instinctively, at the right moment, the birds began to sing a background harmony.

Hesitantly, Timothy began to sing.

Hear the silence growing, in each and every heart.
See the love-glow growing, never to depart.

Wonder filled Timothy's eyes as he sang effortlessly. He took a deep breath and triumphantly sang his gratitude.

I embrace my power, knowing I am free.
Let it be. Let it be!

When Timothy finished, all the animals shouted for more. They whistled and shouted and stomped their feet, shouting and laughing, "More! More!" Maybe they were thinking that if it had taken him a life-time to arrive at the Service of Gratitude, he needs to sing more than one chorus!

Timothy turned and saw the smiling faces of Old John, Cedric, Chandu and Chico. He felt powerful. He felt inspired. He sang the opening verses even louder, and then sang:

I salute the friendship, never to depart.
Let it be. Let it be!

The circle erupted in applause. Timothy looked at Christine. "Do you think they liked it?"

"They loved it," she said. "And they love you. And did you notice something, Timothy? *You did not stutter!*"

"Oh, my Rain-God!" he exclaimed. Followed by a whispered, "Did I say that? I'm so sorry."

Christine smilingly said, "Don't worry. The Rain-God was saying the same!" And they both laughed.

Cedric had hopped out into the center and was about to sing when Toby made a howl of shocked surprise.

"Oh, look. Everybody, look! It's Snake. And he's hurt. He's hurt bad."

The circle opened up and Cedric looked and saw Snake coming towards him. He looked real sick. His skin was wrinkled and bruised. His tongue was hanging at the side of his mouth, but there was no hiss.

Snake was moving but he had lost his power. Snake was sick.

He moved into the center. He moved to be near Cedric. He was afraid. What the animals did not know was that Snake had disappeared because he was ashamed of his sickness. It was ugly. Deforming. It had been afflicting snakes throughout the country for the past four years. Nobody talked about it but all the animals had heard rumours of the 'snake-disease'. Before he disappeared, Snake had had a run-in with some of the animals that drank at the stream; they told him to go away and take his disease with him. He didn't know what to do or where to go. So he'd gone off into the forest to die. For some reason he felt the call to return for the Service of Gratitude. He had arrived in time to hear Cedric sing.

Cedric held Snake closely to him in the center of the circle. They provided a powerful image: a frog hugging a snake so closely to him. Everybody, including the birds, joined to make the background harmony. Cedric sang from the center of his being:

Hear the silence growing, never to depart.
Feel the love-glow growing, in each and every heart.
I embrace the healing, knowing I am free.
Love will never end. Love will never end.

Cedric kissed Snake. Snake was already dead.

Respectfully, and in silence, many of the animals moved forward to pay their respects to Snake. Chandu and Chico hugged him. Most of them said a silent prayer. Some touched him, stroking his body. Some offered the sniff of love. Some gave the sniff of good-bye. And all the time this was happening, Cedric was quietly singing the refrain:

Love will never end.

Love will never end.

Christine flew a hundred feet above the circle. It was a powerful sight. Animals of all descriptions forming a silent line to pay their respects to Snake. Cedric was illuminating a bright white glow that reflected *The Process*. Christine knew that the Spiritual Principles were alive in this community.

She was about to fly back to her new friends when she saw three animals creeping down the hillside. It was Alice, Betty and Irma. They were separating themselves from the circle. Christine's body started to feel weak. She had connected to negativity. Christine *knew* that a dangerous energy was forming within Olde Stable Farm.

The Burial of Snake

Animals do not have an elaborate ceremony for the burial of one of their own. Special friends drag the dead creature to a safe place. Snake was taken to the field at the side of the Hay Barn where the meetings were held. Chandu and Chico requested permission to gently pull Snake to his place of rest. Then came Cedric and Mrs. Ramsbottom, followed by Old John, and the other animals silently joined together in pairs to create a funeral march.

There was no fuss. Very little talk. The birds took the song that Old John had created and harmonized until they reached the place where Snake was to be buried. All the animals who formed the community at Olde Stable Farm were buried in this sacred field.

Mrs. Ramsbottom chose the place where Snake was to be buried. Chandu and Chico used their paws to dig the grave and gently Snake was buried and covered with the warm soil. Everyone came and solemnly looked at the grave, then silently walked away. Nothing was said. No song was sung. The reverent silence said it all.

Within minutes all the animals had moved into the Hay Barn for the regular community meeting. Only Cedric, Chandu and Chico, who had been joined by Christine, remained.

"It was the sickness that killed him," said Chico and Chandu.

"Yes. And there is another sickness that can kill *us*!" said Cedric. He had not planned this prophetic statement and had he been asked what it meant, he wouldn't have known. Fortunately, the other animals just stared at the grave in silence. Cedric then turned and looked at Christine. He knew she understood what he meant.

The Meeting

When Cedric, Chandu, Chico and Christine arrived for the meeting a dispute was taking place between Mrs. Ramsbottom and the chickens. Mrs. Ramsbottom, supported by Old John, felt that because of the death of Snake the meeting should be postponed. However, the chickens, joined by some of the other animals who never attended the Service of Gratitude, felt that it was important for the meeting to take place immediately. They had important information that needed to be shared with all the animals at Olde Stable Farm, and if further deaths were to be avoided, an obvious allusion to Snake's disease, then action needed to be taken. The animals were in an uproar. Many agreed with Mrs. Ramsbottom, but a growing majority joined the chickens.

Cedric called for order. He shouted again. Chandu and Chico joined him in establishing quiet. Mrs.

Ramsbottom, who spoke in slow, deliberate tones, addressed the assembled animals.

"Let us just remember what has happened tonight. Let us remember the praise we expressed at the Service of Gratitude. Let us remember who we are. We are not Big People. Show respect. Respect for the dead. Respect for the living."

The animals felt reprimanded. They knew that Mrs. Ramsbottom disliked noise and needless chatter. She carried a regal dignity at all times.

Cedric broke the nervous silence. "Snake would not want us to miss our meeting. I respectfully suggest, Mrs. Ramsbottom, you call the meeting to order."

Old John, nodding his head, signaled his agreement with Cedric. Mrs. Ramsbottom, swiveling her head in all directions, called the meeting to order.

Alice, Betty and Irma took their positions, ready to address the community. They huddled together to decide who was going to speak. This was not an easy decision to make because they usually spoke at the same time, often contradicting each other. It was decided that Alice would speak for the group with an understanding that the other two could provide information where necessary. After much clucking, Alice was ready to begin.

Alice began to speak in what can only be described as an hypocritically humble tone.

"I acknowledge the most honourable Mrs. Ramsbottom, respected elders, indeed, all members of Olde Stable Farm and beyond. Information has come to me, from numerous sources that I am not able to name at the present time... information has come to me that the sickness that killed Snake was spread to him by... er... I'm sorry to have to say this... er..."

The animals interrupted to demand that she name the spreader.

"Okay, okay," Alice continued. "But I want you to understand that this is not easy for me or my two friends, to say what we know to be true."

Again the animals interrupted. "Name the spreader! Name the spreader!"

"Okay," continued Alice in a sly and obsequious voice. "But it is not one person only. It is two. They are both of a kind. I'm sorry to say this. I'm talking about our two foreign guests. The descendants of Orientals. I'm talking about Chandu and Chico!"

Cedric, taking advantage of the silence, forcefully reminded the meeting, "They are not guests. They were born here. Their families have lived around the farm for many years. They are *not* guests! This is Chandu and Chico's home!"

"Whatever," said Alice.

Mrs. Ramsbottom interjected, "Will you continue, Alice."

Alice took a moment to huddle together with Betty and Irma. Much clucking was heard and then she dramatically brushed her feathers down and stood tall.

"We all know," she continued, "that the relationship between Chandu and Chico is not normal. We are not Big People, and we have no desire to act like them. Animals should not form sexual relationships between their own gender. We know it does happen in extreme cases. Usually when females or males are not around. But the traditions that are handed down from our elders tell us that this is always an unfortunate exception rather than the norm. Nobody here who has children would want them to live the way Chandu and Chico are living."

Many of the other animals murmured their agreement.

Mabel the goose, who spoke with a lisp, and who considered herself a traditionalist, moved closer to Alice to register her support. "Mith Ramthbottom, we all know that what Alith ith thaying ith true. We like Chandu and Chico but by their behaviour, they bring bad luck to our community."

Philip the rooster, who was an angry animal at the best of times, probably because he hated to get up so early in the morning, interjected: "We are experiencing bad luck. No rain for six weeks. No future harvest. The Big People get angry at the drought and they sell many of us off at the markets. This has happened before. Alice is telling us where the bad luck is coming from!"

Chandu and Chico moved closer together. Their fear and sadness at what they were hearing from those they thought to be friends and neighbors were apparent to everyone. What they couldn't see, because their eyes were glued to the speakers at the meeting, was Christine. She was hovering above their heads. Trying desperately to combat the negativity with loving energy.

Alice impatiently flapped her wings. "Snake was a close friend of Chandu and Chico. He was confused about whether he was a he or a she. I have heard that it is the nature of snakes to have that confusion. But don't you think it is a little unusual that an animal who can't decide what he — I mean she — oh dear, it's hard to talk about this he and she business. Help me, Irma. Betty."

Irma moved next to Alice. She had the whiniest cluck on the farm. "Isn't it strange that this sexually confused snake should be close friends with Chandu and Chico? Think about it?"

Betty, who was a plump chicken and spoke only in whispers added, "We know for a fact that last year Snake went and stayed with Chandu and Chico for two days. And that is when he started to get sick."

Alice signaled to Betty and Irma to get back in line. She had pulled herself together, and she knew from experience that once they started to talk, especially with such a grand audience as was gathered for the meeting, they would never shut up.

Alice continued, "We know for a fact that the sickness started after Snake stayed with Chandu and Chico. We also know that Chandu and Chico have broken the animal tradition by living together in a special relationship. Animal law warns us against this behaviour. Where would future animals come from if we all lived like this? Think about it."

Many of the animals were nodding their heads in agreement. "She is making sense," they whispered to each other.

Alice, sensing that many of the animals were in agreement with her, continued in a sly and hypocritical tone. "Mrs. Ramsbottom, we have not spoken to you about this before tonight because we know you are very busy. Very, very busy. Some people say that you are the busiest owl in the kingdom." Alice was being sarcastic.

Mrs. Ramsbottom knew she was being sarcastic. It was part of the folklore at Olde Stable Farm that Mrs. Ramsbottom was very busy. However, nobody knew how this rumour got started. Few creatures had ever seen Mrs. Ramsbottom *do* anything. It was a little like her reputation for wisdom. She was known to be wise, but she rarely ever said anything that anybody remembered. It was just assumed that if you were an owl, you were wise.

It is true that Mrs. Ramsbottom is a good listener. She had the ear of everybody and she could keep a secret. Nobody could ever accuse Mrs. Ramsbottom of being a gossip. But she rarely said anything. People would talk for hours to her and she would simply say, "Oh, yes," or "Oh, no," or "Oh, dear!" Animals went to ask for advice and usually talked *themselves* into a solution.

Mrs. Ramsbottom glared at Alice, as only an owl can glare. She turned her head around three or more times so that Alice began to feel nauseous and said, in her most stately tone, "Yes. Yes. Please continue."

"Thank you," said Alice. Gradually gaining her composure she continued. "We have not spoken to you about this Mrs. Ramsbottom. And we have never talked about it at this community meeting, but I — I mean, *we* — " Looking in the direction of Betty and Irma, she continued. "We have talked with many of the animals. We've even talked with animals who live on other farms. Everybody that we've talked to believes that the sickness that killed Snake came from Chandu and Chico."

A loud gasp burst from many of the animals who were still loyal friends of Chandu and Chico. Chico closed his eyes and tightly hugged Chandu. He prayed to the Rain-God, "Let this be a bad dream. Let me open my eyes and see that I have been sleeping." He slowly opened his eyes to see the feather head, beady eyes and sharp beak of Alice looking right at him.

"We will have no luck until we remove Chandu and Chico from Olde Stable Farm. It will not rain until we take action. *For the sake of the many it is sometimes necessary that a few should suffer!*"

Irma clucked, "Their behaviour is not in keeping with the family life-style we wish to encourage at Olde Stable Farm. They are dangerous to our childrens' future behaviour and health. Let's face it, they are dangerous to all of us. How can any of us eat or drink with such animals who spread a deadly disease?"

"It is with a sense of genuine sadness," said Alice in her most dramatic and theatrical chicken-style, knowing that the animals were listening to every word that fell from her beak, "that I recommend, tonight, that Chandu and Chico be banished from Olde Stable Farm!"

There was a hushed silence as Alice finished her recommendation, broken by a spasmodic applause from various parts of the Hay Barn. It was difficult to see who applauded, but most seemed to be nodding in agreement.

Christine beamed her energy to Chandu and Chico as the meeting slowly evolved into a trial. They were huddled together desperately trying to comfort each other as the harangue proceeded, not really knowing what to do. Cedric knew he had to say something but he wanted Alice to finish her series of accusations.

Christine flew to Cedric's side. She knew he was about to speak and she also knew he was afraid. Unsure about what words to use. Consumed by the seriousness of events that were unfolding before his eyes. He felt that the fate of Chandu and Chico was resting upon his shoulders. Christine did something that she had learned from Genesis: She made the present stand still. Because time as we know it does not exist in the life of an angel, she was able to make everything freeze until she had spoken to Cedric. Only when Cedric was ready to address the meeting would the earth-time be reactivated.

"Cedric, I must speak with you," said Christine. "First you must relax and connect with all that I have told you about the Spiritual Principles. They are a process. And they are to be discovered in this meeting. Remember I said that the seekers are about bringing Insight, Wisdom and Harmony to this planet. Gary Zukav and others are trying to do this with the Big People, and you are about to move into The Process here on Olde Stable Farm. You are discovering who you *are*. The sadness, gloom and depression that was haunting you before our meeting will be no more so long as you focus upon The Process. You are a seeker. This is who you are.

"Remember, those who have been speaking are coming from their place of pain. Remember that. They speak from *their* pain. It is not really about Chandu and Chico. Or about the death of Snake. They are afraid, confused, insecure... here's that word again,... *disconnected*... and they lash out at the unusual, the different, strange, those who they see as foreigners. They blame others for the pain that lives in their souls. Pain is their soul-sickness."

Cedric felt weak. He felt the same powerlessness and gloom that he was feeling when Christine plopped into the pond. The Process alone couldn't stop the megrims and vapours from returning. In real life, nothing lasts forever. Bad things happen. He had known this before and never knew how to deal with it.

Dejectedly, he asked Christine, "How can they say such terrible things about Chandu and Chico? Snake's death is bad enough but now we must endure this. It is so horrid. No wonder Oscar Whatshisname called it a love that could not be spoken. And to think that we are still putting people on trial because their loving is not the same as ours. Mrs. Ramsbottom is friendly with Rebecca, the owl who lives in East Grinstead. They take vacations together. Will Mrs. Ramsbottom be next? How can they twist the fact that we have not had rain for six weeks with Chandu and Chico's relationship? They manipulate fear and feed our most basic prejudices. What they are saying is not right. I must say something. I canot stand by and let this happen!"

Christine looked directly into Cedric's eyes and he felt a warm glow in his tummy. He felt a calmness developing in every part of his body as Christine firmly responded.

"It is tempting to seek to answer each of their accusations and try to *prove* that what they are saying or feeling is wrong. That they are misinterpreting the ancient tradition. That they do not understand the Spiritual Principles. You can get dragged into the dangerous game of Point and Counterpoint.

"Cedric, you must hear what I am saying. What is happening here is almost an exact replica of the abusiveness that is separating and destroying the Big People. Until they deal with the pain that exists in their own individual souls, there can be no healing.

"This is also true for the animals who live here at Olde Stable Farm. The seekers are called to be healers. We must Heal the pain that continues to divide and separate us. This is... this is The Process of the More."

Cedric said, "But we cannot allow the innocent to suffer."

"Cedric, seek to take this meeting back to the atmosphere that all the animals created with the Rain-God on Jacob's Hill. The Service of Gratitude must be more than words, prayers and spiritual songs.

Those wonderful affirmations need to become behaviors and actions. The Word must again become flesh. Remember my conversation with you in the cottage. Discover the meaning *behind* the words. *Touch* the pain and insecurity that exists behind the accusations of Alice, Betty and Irma. Bring harmony to the meeting.

"Oh, yes, don't worry about Chandu and Chico. I am with them. They have each other. Speak for yourself, Cedric."

Christine flew back to Chandu and Chico, and unstopped time. Cedric hopped next to Mrs. Ramsbottom. He was ready to speak.

The Process

"Members of Olde Stable Farm. I am not here to speak for Chandu and Chico. They are more than capable of representing themselves. I am here to speak for myself.

"Many of you saw my new friend, the angel Christine, arrive with Timothy at the Service of Gratitude tonight. I have not been her friend for a very long time, but time means nothing to an angel. Before I met her at Tunbridge Pond, I was feeling extremely hop-less. I had a severe bout of the megrims and vapours. My life seemed to have little meaning.

It was hard for many of the animals to imagine Cedric feeling hop-less. They began to murmur among themselves in shocked surprise. "Cedric... feeling hop-less. Possibly suicidal?" He always appeared happy and confident. Always doing for others. Nothing was too much trouble. He was extremely popular, more popular than he could ever realize, with more friends than he knew what to do with. He even had a special friendship with Muriel. Most animals would willingly exchange a wing or hoof for Cedric's life, although few would want to look like him! He was loved by everybody. He was the gentlefrog of Tunbridge Pond.

"Please let me finish. I felt hop-less because I was disconnected. Yes, I had friends. I have few worries. I attend the Service of Gratitude and I enjoy singing. But... I felt the pain of disconnection. I knew deep inside my soul that there were problems at the Farm, problems around Tunbridge Pond and problems with many of my friends and neighbours."

Cedric looked directly at Alice, Betty and Irma, and gently smiled at them. "I was particularly aware of Snake's sickness. I was aware of all these things. I felt them and yet I did not have the courage to talk about them. The great William Snakespit has his character Falstaff say to Oliver Crockwell, *Remember, Oliver, it is the beginning of bedlam when two people cannot communicate.* I was talking, but not really communicating. There was no connection. I made myself feel special by quoting from history and literature, but deep down I felt small and unimportant. An insignificant little frog.

"I was happy when I made all of you happy. I hated disagreements and so I hopped all over Tunbridge Pond and Olde Stable Farm making you feel good. But inside

I often felt by myself. Mrs. Ramsbottom put her claw on it when she said that I didn't appreciate who I really am. I remember exactly what you said. 'Friends are important, but you are essential.' For most of my life I saw myself as an insignificant little frog.

"The sickness that we have all called Snake-disease has been around for a long time and it does not just affect snakes! That is simply a myth. My mother, who was definitely not a snake, died with the same symptoms. Her skin had lesions and was bruised. She had no energy. It was the same. The difference between Snake and my mother was that she had a family to take care of her before she died. There are more than fifty of my family who live around Tunbridge Pond, that's not including those who moved away. Probably while I've been speaking here twenty more relatives have been born!" Some of the animals laughed at this remark. Others smiled and nodded their heads in agreement. Frogs were known to be prolific; they made up in numbers what they lacked in size.

"Snake was *alone*. Few here saw my mother the weeks before she died. She was cared for, in seclusion, at the house near Lily Bend. Snake, always a loner, had nobody to nurse him. He tried to deal with the sickness in full view of all of us. And believe me, this disease, because it looks so horrid and we feel so helpless, makes everyone afraid."

Cedric could not resist his next remark. "Irma, if I'm not mistaken, you said that the same disease had taken a sister and a cousin. Most of us remember the tragic circumstances that surrounded the death of your sister. The pain. The helplessness."

Irma did not know what to do with herself. She felt the piercing eyes of Alice and Betty but at the same time the mention of her sister, the pain and helplessness that surrounded her death, it was all creating feelings of sadness. Tears rolled down the side of her beak. How could she ever forget her loving sister Iris.

"Yes, I remember, Cedric. You were kind to me during that awful time. Yes, I remember," said Irma.

Christine noticed that Chandu and Chico were sitting apart, together in their separateness, but glowing with an energy of confidence. Cedric was also glowing. He had found his way to The Process.

"Let me say something about my dear friends Chandu and Chico. I know that they are different. When I first met them and saw their love — Alice, I want you to know that I saw love, nothing more! I felt a little awkward. Two male cats obviously in love with each other. But they never hid it. They were never offensive in my presence. Sure, they hugged and kissed each other but they also hugged and kissed me. Probably all of us in this Hay Barn have experienced a Burmese hug!

"Soon I realized that my awkwardness was not about them. It was about *me*. Again, I felt the pain that lies at the center of my own soul. The disconnection. How could I feel awkward around love and affection?

"If it was natural for them to have loved females I'm sure they would have done so. Most of us know their families. Yet Chandu and Chico are not like their parents. They know they can never have children. They know that some people gossip behind their backs. And yet they have chosen to remain at Olde Stable Farm. Everybody here has experienced their generosity. Their gentle play. Their affection.

"Also, just look at the health that radiates from them both. Clean... fresh beautiful bodies, bright smiling eyes and gorgeous fur. Just look at the shine. The glow."

It was absolutely true. Chandu and Chico were very attractive. Chandu was a Burmese blue. Chico was sable. Both had excellent physiques. Even Roger the Fox, when he first arrived at the Farm, had been attracted to Chico. However, nobody could ever separate or disconnect the energy that existed between Chandu and Chico."

Christine thought to herself, as she listened to Cedric: "If the Olde Stable Farm community could only see it, here is a model relationship being demonstrated before their eyes."

Cedric was really glowing now. Words were coming to him as he needed them. "Let me tell you about the time that Snake stayed with Chandu and Chico. *I* arranged that. I had asked Snake if he wanted to come and stay with me at the cottage but he felt it would be too far from his friends at the Farm. He wanted to be near Chandu and Chico. They had never made fun about his gender confusion. They helped him to feel comfortable with himself. Snake wanted to be near them but was too ashamed, because of his physical condition, to ask them. So I went to see Chandu and Chico and they were overjoyed to have Snake stay with them. Chico spent hours collecting fresh straw and washing down the wood that provided shelter."

Turning to Alice, Cedric continued, "Winston Churchill said that a little knowledge is a dangerous thing. You would do well to remember this. Snake was already sick when he went to stay with Chandu and Chico. That's the reason he went to stay with them.

"Also, they would never tell you but Chandu and Chico were prepared to nurse him till he died. They wanted to be his family. But as we all know... Snake was a loner. He held onto his pain right to the end."

Tears were streaming down everyone's face. The Hay Barn was beginning to glow.

John

Old John stepped forward. He had not talked with Christine. He did not know about The Process or the Spiritual Principles. But he connected to Cedric's use of the word *pain*. He knew something about love and pain!

Old John was the senior resident at Olde Stable Farm. He had all the characteristics that we associate with a mule. He could be stubborn. He was slow. He did not speak often but when he did everyone listened. Old John was respected. When he moved forward into the silence that followed Cedric's speech the whole community was attentive.

"You all know that I am not a speaker. I don't know 'bout you, but I'm still in mourning for Snake. I didn't know him as well as some of you, but I felt his pain. My sadness is that I never shared with him what I am about to tell you." Old John walked around and looked pensively at Alice, Betty and Irma. Then he walked over and smiled at Chandu and Chico.

"I was once in love with a beautiful mule called Elizabeth. She lived on the Farm. For a while we were the only mules here." He cast his eyes over the community that was assembled and focused for a moment on the group of mules that were standing immediately behind the chickens.

"I loved Elizabeth. But I couldn't tell her my true feelings. She could talk better than me. She used words I didn't understand. I never felt good enough for her. She wanted me to say something. Something that would make her feel good. I didn't know the right words. So I didn't say anything. Just clammed up like a stupid mule. I was too stubborn to ask for help.

"When the other mules started to arrive she got friendly with Arnold. I knew she didn't love him the way she loved me but he could speak his affection for her. For more than a year she waited for me. I couldn't even tell her that I loved her. We don't say stuff like that in my family. 'Specially men. Talking about love is girl stuff.

"When I saw Elizabeth with Arnold it made me sick. I hated the sight of him. Then I started getting angry at her. It was a mess. I was in a bad mood all the time, and pouted around like a baby. I did stupid stuff. Once I butted Arnold for no reason. I even tried to kick him. He just ran away. But Elizabeth was afraid. She said I was getting violent.

"One night Elizabeth came to see me. Arnold wanted to be with her. He wanted something special. She asked me what I thought. I told her to do what she wanted. They deserved each other. I was mad. I said awful mean things to her. Inside I was screaming, *Please don't leave me. I love you. I can make you happy.* But to her face I just told her to go on, I didn't need her.

"She walked away that evening. She kept turning and looking at me. I guess she was hoping I'd call her back. I turned my head and wouldn't look at her. She walked into the night and I've not seen her since."

Old John stood silent for a moment. Then he moved and looked at Chandu and Chico. "I admire *you* both very much. You show your love and don't seem to care what others think about you. I admire you. You have a love that you can show.

"I used to think that I didn't understand your kind of love. But that is not true. Love is love. None of us loves the same way. We are different, even those who belong to the same breed. Our love is different but it is the same. "

Continuing to speak directly to Chandu and Chico, Old John continued, "I was jealous of your love. I hated the way you could kiss, hug and laugh in front of the other animals. I imagined that it was Elizabeth and me. But then I'd come back to earth. I was alone.

"I watched you both when Alice was speaking. Please try not to get upset by what you heard. You are not the cause of this trouble. You both loved Snake. Snake loved you. Your love helped him feel better. " Old John paused, searching for the right words.

"Take it from me. It don't matter how much you love if you can't say it. You gotta show 'em. You gotta tell 'em. That's what you guys do. You're not afraid to show your love. And I think that makes people different when they're around you. Snake was different when he was with you. I know I feel different inside when I'm with you." Old John smiled fondly at the cats, who sat hugging each other, smiling through their tears.

Old John took another deep breath. He rarely spoke more than a few sentences at a time, and he had never spoken with such heartfelt emotion. "I was afraid to show my love, and so I felt stupid when I was with Elizabeth. When I'd feel stupid for not knowing the fancy love-words, I'd get angry at Elizabeth. But when I'm with you two, I'm not afraid. You're showing me how to love. I think that's what scares the others. They don't know how to show love. So they get angry and make showing love wrong." Cedric, Timothy and Muriel nodded in agreement.

"Please stick around. Don't let them chase you away. We need you. We need you to show us how to love." In his deep soulful voice, Old John then started to sing what he had sung during the Gratitude Service, only now it took on a deeper meaning.

Hear the silence growing, in each and every heart.
See the love-glow growing, never to depart.
We are ONE together, knowing we are free.
Let it be. Let it be.

Timothy, who had remained silent throughout the meeting, picked up on the refrain:

Hear the silence growing, in each and every heart.

Soon all the animals, with the exception of Alice, Betty and Irma, Mabel the goose and Philip the rooster, who left before Old John finished speaking, joined Timothy in the song and the Hay Barn was aglow. Nothing more was said that evening. Mrs. Ramsbottom closed the meeting with the wise words, "Let us all go home and get some rest."

And the animals responded, "Peace." At that moment, it started to rain.

The Kiss

When Cedric woke up it was still early but late for him. He was usually up before the Sun but on this morning the sun had already started its journey.

"Good morning, Christine," said Cedric. "Or as St. Francis said to Sissi, *Praise to thee, my Lord of all creatures. Above us Brother Sun who brings us the day and lends us his light.*"

"Oh, you're awake. Good morning, Cedric," said Christine.

"Christine," said Cedric, "I didn't thank you for your advice before I spoke to the meeting last night. What you said made a great deal of sense. I know *you knew* I was going to say something in defense of Chandu and Chico but what I was going to say was so different from what I actually said.

"I was going to criticize Alice. It was all I could do to stop myself from hopping on her beak when she was talking. That gossiping trio is always up to mischief. But you quietly reminded me that little is achieved if we only exchange venom with venom. — Oops, sorry, Snake, wherever you are!" And they both laughed.

"I'm very proud of you, " said Christine. "You did an excellent job. I also know that Genesis is proud of what you said. And the courage you showed in doing it."

Cedric was beginning to glow. He was beginning to love himself. More than that, he was beginning to make a connection with The Process. The Spiritual Principles of Insight, Wisdom and Harmony were coming alive in his life. He was on the journey that Mrs. Ramsbottom had spoken about before he had me Christine: an appreciation of Cedric.

He continued, "When you used the word pain to describe what is really going on with Alice, Betty and Irma, I was able to understand them. Instead of them becoming the enemy, they became fellow sufferers of a pain that affects all of us at times. God knows I felt that pain just before I met you. Remember me telling you."

"Yes," said Christine. "I didn't forget."

"Sorry," said Cedric. Again, they laughed.

"You know," said Christine. "Angels also have pain. I told you about the love I had for a man in a previous life who didn't love me. But there have been other times when I felt empty, and yes, hop-less. When

I was training with Genesis, I didn't think that I would ever be good enough to be a proper angel. I made so many mistakes. Once I was helping a woman who was being beaten by her husband. I thought it was my job to keep them together. One night he nearly killed her. I felt it was all my fault. I went to Genesis and told him. I was throwing in my wings. I was a failure.

"In his raspy voice, pulling on his earring, he simply said, *Fine. But how does your giving up help that woman? Maybe it is the woman who should give up the husband.*

"At that moment I made a connection with Insight. Sometimes, we must love somebody enough to walk away. An angel's job is not to fix people but seek to show The Process.

"That is what Mrs. Ramsbottom did last night. She allowed the meeting to evolve into The Process. She did not interfere or try to make anything happen. Rather —"

"She never interferes," interrupted Cedric. "She lets people say what they need to say and usually things work out for the best. Mrs. Ramsbottom is... not disconnected but the other word. Detached. That's what she is."

Christine glowed bright yellow. "Genesis once told me about an Archangel whose motto for living was detachment."

"Maybe Mrs. Ramsbottom is a fallen Archangel," laughed Cedric.

Christine laughed with him. "Maybe. Maybe. Who knows? Shall we have some breakfast?"

"I've got some lily leaves to eat. I don't think that they are as tasty as fresh grass, but they're a lot better than plant-roots. Don't tell Muriel I said that!"

Christine smiled. "You know I really like you, Cedric. You are a special frog."

Cedric blushed behind his yellow, green and brown skin. "I like you, too!"

Nothing was said for a few moments. Cedric suddenly sensed that Christine would be leaving him soon.

"When will you be going?" Cedric asked wistfully.

"Soon. Soon I will continue my journey to Paradise. But I will never leave you. Once you have met an angel the *connection* never goes away. It's like love. Once you love somebody it never dies." As Christine was saying this she fluttered close to Cedric's face and kissed him.

Immediately, Cedric began to glow. Energy flowed from his body and he felt... he felt... blessed. He had used that word a few times and had heard Old John and Mrs. Ramsbottom use the word in the Service of Gratitude. But he had never felt it. When Christine kissed him he *felt* blessed.

"Now," said Christine. "Let's eat the lily leaves."

Sophia

Christine summoned Genesis while she was eating the lily leaves. "Who is Mrs. Ramsbottom?" she asked. "I'm sure you are keeping something from me."

Genesis had expected this conversation but not quite so soon. He had been resting and so his voice sounded more like scratchy sandpaper than usual. "Your intuitive process has been working overtime, I see. So you have recognized Sophia. That's what she was called before she took the form of an owl. Little Cedric was right. She is indeed an Archangel. Actually, an ex-Archangel. She resigned."

"What?" Christine was astonished. "She resigned? How can she do that?"

"She did," shrugged Genesis. "She had a disagreement with THE ONE WHO KNOWS and she resigned. "

"What was it about?" Christine was sure it had to be something truly cataclysmic.

"Detachment. Sophia felt that the ultimate expression of The Process is detachment. Loving enough not to get involved. She felt that the only way creatures would evolve to spiritual responsibility is through standing back and letting The Process work."

"Oh, so *she's* the Archangel who lived detachment!" Christine was astonished. Then she said half-joking, "But she couldn't have been all *that* detached if she actually argued with THE ONE WHO KNOWS. Wow. I've never heard of anyone daring to argue with the Big O.W.K.!" Christine exclaimed.

"Oh, it's happened before," Genesis continued. "In the early days a number of angels felt that they knew more than THE ONE WHO KNOWS. However, their motives were not pure. They wanted more control. In the case of Sophia, she felt that less was more. The less involvement, the more chance The Process had of working. The big blow-up came when she was working with a revolutionary called Moses. Sophia felt that there should be no special effects: no ball of fire, no famine, no parting of the Red Sea. No tablets magically inscribed in stone.

"She was always arguing for detachment. THE ONE WHO KNOWS felt that the Big People needed a sign. Anyway, their disagreements continued with the adventures of Buddha, the early Church, some Hindus, Mohammed and other spiritual teachers.

"Then one day she asked if she could be released from her duties and manifest as a regular creature. It was her request, and THE ONE WHO KNOWS granted it."

"You mean she went from being an Archangel to... to being an owl?" Christine was totally flabbergasted.

"That's exactly what I mean," said Genesis. "Before she became Mrs. Ramsbottom, she has been a horse, an elephant... I think for a time she was a gorilla in Africa. Always with detachment. Interestingly, Sophia has never asked to be a Big Person, even a miniature one like you."

"Is THE ONE WHO KNOWS angry with her?" Christine asked.

"What a silly question. Of course not. He granted her request. Variety is the spice of Paradise." Genesis smiled to himself, pulling at his ear. "In fact, I think THE ONE WHO KNOWS is slowly coming to the conclusion that Sophia might have been right all the time. It gets to be complicated when we involve ourselves in the affairs of creatures. Although it sometimes means that creatures get hurt when we choose not to interfere, detachment nurtures a more respectful understanding of The Process."

"How am I to treat her?" asked Christine.

"With detachment," said Genesis, grinning. "Now return to your adventures. Cedric is becoming restless. He thinks you are not enjoying his lily-leaves."

Timothy

Christine chewed on her lily-leaves and out of the blue, she began to think about Timothy. Perhaps it was triggered by the conversation with Genesis about detachment. Timothy, by the circumstances of his inability to move efficiently and his stutter, had developed his own unusual form of detachment. "I would like to spend some time with Timothy," she said. "Shall we go and find him?"

"That would be wonderful. I know he would love to see you again before you go," said Cedric.

"Maybe we can arrange a supper before I leave," said Christine. "It would be a time of *connection* with my special friends. Also, Muriel would have an excuse to feast on her favorite plant-roots."

They laughed. Cedric was about to ask who Christine would like at the supper, but suddenly, he *knew*.

"I shall invite Muriel, Old John, Timothy, Roger and Toby."

"Exactly," said Christine.

"When?" said Cedric.

"We will know. We *all* will know. Trust The Process," said Christine.

"I hope this doesn't sound too stupid, but what exactly *is* The Process?" asked Cedric.

Christine flew closely towards Cedric and was hovering directly in front of his nose, staring intently into his eyes. He did not have a copyright on drama. "Genesis says there are no stupid questions. Silly ones, certainly. I've been guilty of a few of them. But not stupid ones. If you don't understand something, it's smart to ask. Hopefully the answer will help you figure out the confusion. Rarely is there an all-embracing answer that doesn't require some work on your part. Remember, we're on a journey. An adventure. We are discovering new possibilities all the time."

As she said this, Christine was reminded of her conversation concerning Sophia and THE ONE WHO KNOWS. The Process. The adventure. New possibilities also embraced THE ONE WHO KNOWS. Christine found this insight to be comforting and a momentary glow shone from her body.

"A wonderful example of The Process is what you did at the Hay Barn meeting. Initially, you wanted to vent your frustration on Alice and some of the other animals, but you took time to hear me. That's Insight.

"Then you used what I said to develop a theme that addressed the community's fear and pain about snake-disease. You gently provided facts that nurtured change. That's Wisdom.

"This allowed the residents, with a few exceptions, to come together. Harmony. The Process is not about having all the answers or being perfect. It's more about living the adventure with integrity."

Stretching out his arms to birth a famous quote, Cedric said that William Snakespit was insightful when he proclaimed that the world is a stage and we are the players. The trick is not to take ourselves too seriously.

"Exactly, said Christine. "Now, let's go and see Timothy."

Timothy was waiting to go somewhere, or was returning from having been somewhere when he suddenly saw Cedric hopping towards him and Christine hovering above Cedric's head. He was so excited he didn't know what to do and so he started going around in a circle. When they are confused or excited, snails often go around in circles.

"G-Good to see you, Cedric. Oh, Christine, I g-get to see you again!" said Timothy.

"Hi, Hello-Goodnight. How are you?" said Cedric.

Christine flew very close to him so that he felt her love.

"I'm s-still sh-shaking after last n-night. I f-feel af-fraid," said Timothy.

"That's why I wanted to visit you," said Christine. "You showed great courage last night because we were with you. But I knew this morning you would be afraid."

"Oh, I'm s-so p-pleased that you came to s-see me. Christine, wh-when I w-was w-with you I d-did not s-stutter. Remember? *You* c-cured me of my s-stuttering. And even if I'm s-stuttering today I know what it w-was like — even if it w-was only th-that one night — not to s-stutter! You have g-given me something that I will cherish all the d-days of my life."

Cedric interjected, "That's what happens when you are with an angel. Things happen. Things change. "

"Yes, but… " Christine said.

"It's true, it's really true!" continued Cedric.

"Timothy, if I were to tell you all that has happened to us since Christine came into our lives it would blow the shell off your back."

"Aaah! Don't say th-that!" said Timothy.

"Sorry. Only a manner of speaking. Don't take it personally!" said Cedric.

"Okay, I won't," said Timothy.

"Where was I…? Yes, it's really true. All the animals that met Christine have changed in some way," said Cedric.

"Okay. Let's just sit down and talk about something," said Christine.

"An angel only reflects what is already there. Think about it this way. I reflect back to you what is already inside you."

"You sound like a mirror," said Timothy.

"That's exactly right," said Christine. "I learned this from Genesis, who was my teacher in Paradise. Another word for messenger is angel. The seekers' journey is to become their own angel."

"I was able to help you and Cedric because you wanted help. Connection requires two willing energies. I only reflected back to you what your soul longed for — and when the time was right you became a seeker."

"Then why I am s-still af-fraid?"

"Because there is much in life to fear," continued Christine. "At the risk of sounding like a preacher, there is a difference in being afraid and living in fear."

"That's me," said Timothy.

"For today," said Christine. "But you have tasted The Process and you will never forget that experience. It is this connection that reminds you of what you are capable of *feeling*, what you are capable of *being*.

"Just remember that wonderful evening Timothy, and see what you did to co-create the journey away from fear. You agreed to let me carry you through the air to Jacob's Hill. You wanted to sing in the center of the circle. And when John had finished his song at the community meeting, it was *you* who got everybody to sing.

"Timothy, your stutter disappeared when *you* embraced The Process and discovered the More."

Cedric listened and started to glow. He understood what Christine was saying. Indeed he, as a frog, had lived it. The feelings he was having now were reminiscent of his days as a tadpole. He remembered when the day came when he needed to change, and he was afraid. He didn't know what was happening to him but he felt that it was his destiny. He was becoming a frog. And even on his worst days he would never want to go back to being a tadpole. In a similar way he knew he would not regret the changes that were taking place within him since his first meeting with Christine."

"I'm enjoying this buh-but c-can we rest?" said Timothy. "I know we haven't buh-been anywhere but all this t-talk about the P-Process makes me tired. C-Can we just sit and look at each other?"

"That sounds like a great idea," said Christine.

"Okay by me," said Cedric. He was glad to have the opportunity to think more about becoming a seeker.

Christine gave a glance towards Cedric. He knew she knew what he was thinking.

Toby

They had not been resting for very long when they were awakened by a noise of an animal in great pain. It was the unmistakable sound of a dog yelping frantically. It was the sound of Toby.

As Cedric, Timothy and Christine gathered together to locate where the sound of pain was coming from they saw Toby running madly in all directions, turning in circles at one moment, biting his tail at the next and then biting into the air. It was an acrobatic vision that would have been an incredible performance, had it not been accompanied by yelps of pain. Quite a show. It was not long before the vision became tragically clear.

Toby was surrounded by a swarm of wasps. Everybody knew that Toby was known for never being still, except when he slept. Even then he was a nervous sleeper who would jump and yelp throughout the night. He tended to face life nose first. He had no boundaries. He was always banging into things, running enthusiastically into any group of animals that he knew, always looking for company — for about two minutes — then running off to find something or somebody else to irritate. Nothing at Olde Stable Farm or around Tunbridge Pond was safe from Toby's nose. It went into everything. However, today he had gone too far. He had put his sniffing nose into a wasp hole!

The wasps resented interference from other animals, and they tended to keep to themselves. As long as the animals left them alone things were fine but if they were disturbed, especially by a wet-sniffing sheepdog nose, all hell would break loose. And it had.

What could be done? Very little. When it had happened before, the offending animal would either take refuge in the waters of Tunbridge Pond or seek to outrun the army of attacking wasps. Toby had tried to outrun the wasps, but had clearly lost the race.

Also, he was hurt. In his enthusiasm to explore new territory he had pushed his nose completely into the wasp hole. He had so much fun barking and playing at the entrance that he didn't hear the angry buzz of protest his nose had triggered. Toby's perpetual excitment always blinded him to his surroundings. He hadn't even noticed the wasp squadron flying around the entrance, guarding against invasion. Until they dive-bombed his backside, left tantalizingly exposed by his wagging tail.

Poor Toby. He looked like a double-ended wasp hive, as the furious wasps had gone straight for the only spots not protected by fur: his nose and rear-end. The wasps who couldn't get a swipe at bare flesh launched kamikaze raids against his middle, hurling themselves stinger-first into his thick fur. "Take that, you nosy, gallumphing clod. Take that! And that! And that!"

Christine wasted no time. She also knew that what she was about to do could be dangerous. For her journey back to Paradise she had chosen to manifest herself in the form of a small Big Person with wings. That meant that her skin was vulnerable to attack. Still, she was determined to stop this massacre of Toby.

Within seconds she had flown into the center of the marauding wasps. She was one amongst hundreds. Summoning all the energy that she had stored within herself during her training with Genesis, she turned this energy into a piercing whine that only the wasps could hear. Quickly, she tuned it so high it shattered the wasps' hearing. It was all that the wasps could do to stay in the same space as Christine and within moments they had backed off Toby and were retreating to the safety of their hole. Only one wasp had managed to attack Christine whilst she was summoning up the sound-energy — but one sting was enough, even for an angel. Christine felt the itching pain and had greater insight into what Toby must be feeling.

Cedric and Timothy looked at each other. "Th-Thank G-God it's over," said Timothy.

"Oh, Toby. Poor Toby. Come over here. Come over and rest," Cedric called.

Toby was still attacking phantom wasps and at the same time licking the sting bites.

"Dear Rain-God! The pain is awful! Those nasty little insects. No wonder they have no friends. They deserve each other. Who would have thought that a friendly greeting would have produced such a response. It's not as if they were still asleep and I'd wakened them up! Ouch! Oh, my dear Rain-God, they even found my butt to sting. And everyone knows that I have the smallest butt on the Farm! They even stung my butt! Ouch! The pain is awful. My poor nose!"

Cedric and Timothy tried to hide their laughter. The thought of wasps attacking a sheepdog's butt was funny. Sometimes the funniest things come from hearing about the things we rarely talk about, and hearing about them in a different context. Whoever heard of a sheepdog's butt being attacked by wasps!

Christine was hovering close to Timothy. She had licked her sting-bite and it was already healing.

"Come here," said Christine. "Try to sit and rest."

"I can't sit. Not for the moment," said Toby. "It seems as if my nose and butt are swelling into the size of Betsy."

"They are," said Cedric.

Again everybody laughed. Even Toby. Betsy the pig was often the recipient of fat-jokes. Although she never seemed to take offense, there must have been times when her feelings were hurt. However, Betsy was partly responsible because she was the first to make fun of her humongous size. Christine heard the reference to Betsy and experienced a *connection* that she had felt before when her name had been mentioned. She knew they needed to meet. Christine instinctively knew that Betsy was to be involved in the future adventures of Olde Stable Farm, and that she was a seeker.

"Thank you for rescuing me, Christine," said Toby. "Thank you so much. I don't know what I'd have done if you hadn't been here at exactly the right time. What a coincidence." The word coincidence had been mentioned again.

As Toby said this he was licking and scratching every part of his body. He had taken on a comical appearance with his nose and butt swelling up.

"That's what happens when you run around in a mad fashion. I can't tell you how many times you have squashed me with your paws. You did it again before the Service of Gratitude. You don't mean to do it. You just don't think about what you are doing. Where you are standing or putting your nose. You stick your nose into everything and everybody's business. You've been doing this for years. How many times have you heard it said that Toby rushes in where angels fear to tread?" said Cedric.

He thought for a moment and then looked at Christine. They both smiled at each other and laughed. That saying had now come alive, literally.

"M-maybe it's a g-good th-thing that I don't rush anywhere. Or even g-go anywhere. K-keeps me out of t-trouble!" said Timothy.

Christine stroked Timothy's head gently. "Let's not forget balance. Things don't have to be one extreme or the other. Happiness is usually found somewhere in the middle."

"Oh, I'm not that bad," said Toby. He wasn't really thinking about what he was saying because he was too busy trying to keep his body from swelling before his very eyes. But he didn't have to think about saying, "Oh, I'm not that bad," because he said it all the time.

"Oh yes, you are th-that buh-bad," said Timothy. "It wasn't th-that long ago you visited m-me for b-barely two minutes and in th-that short t-time you nearly k-killed me. You know what I'm t-talking about. You were in such a hurry to g-get to me you k-kicked m-me against the t-tree and I landed on a rock. I th-thought you'd smashed my shell. And without my shell I would g-get sick and d-die. I really was afraid. I th-thought you'd smashed my shell!"

Toby was just about to say that it wasn't that bad when Timothy continued, "And you were afraid, t-too, T-Toby. You k-kept apologizing. You licked me d-down a hundred t-times in the t-two minutes you were with me. F-First you smashed me against a t-tree and then you nearly d-drowned me!"

Although it was serious, the animals had to laugh. Even Christine was beginning to enjoy the whimsical humor that surrounded the lives of these animals.

"Th-Thank G-God you don't c-come to see me t-too often," continued Timothy.

"You're always in a hurry," said Cedric.

"Where are you going?" said Christine. "If you are always in a hurry where are you trying to get to? Where are you going?"

That question caught Toby by surprise. For years people had told him about how he stuck his nose into places he shouldn't, and that he was always in a hurry. He didn't seem to stay any place for more than a few minutes. Even when he attended the Service of Gratitude he was restless. Looking around and sniffing all the other animals. The animals liked Toby but he was a nuisance. He was his worst enemy. He caused his own problems.

"Where are you going?" Christine continued to ask this question.

Christine understood that she could help the seekers not just by asking the right questions. It was about *how* she asked those questions and *when* she asked them. Language creates spiritual awareness through energy and timing. When energy is only connected with actions and feeling and is not used in the creation of words, all real conversation is lost. What creates the *experience* is not just the selection of words, but how we phrase them, and the energy that we give them in their delivery. Timing — when to embrace the silence and when to break it — is part of what creates *connection*. Christine had become a master of knowing when to ask the questions and how to ask the questions and what energy to place within each word.

"Where are you going?" she asked again.

"I really don't know," said Toby.

Cedric and Timothy had a feeling that this conversation could take a long time, so they both sat down. This was not hard for Timothy to do since he was always sitting.

"Let's approach it another way," said Christine. "Do you think you should be going somewhere in your life? Is there a meaning to life that should determine our actions, behavior and personality."

"What do you mean, determine?" said Toby.

"Being responsible" said Christine. "Are you responsible for the life you live and the situations you create? Or do things just happen?"

"Give me a moment to think," said Toby. He was still scratching and licking his wounds but Christine definitely had his attention.

"While you are thinking I want you to listen to a story, " said Christine.

"A giant, who lived alone, built a huge wall around his house. He also placed signs saying, *Please do not ring the bell* and *Do not climb the walls*. Not content with having the wall and the signs he bought two huge fierce-looking guard dogs to protect his property.

"Alone in the house he would have conversations with himself that went like this: *Why do I have no friends? Nobody ever invites me to their home for dinner. It's been years since I went to a party. When will anybody ever visit me? I'm so lonely*."

"Toby, this is only a story but it has a message for everybody. Who was creating the giant's pain?"

"The stupid giant, of course," said Toby. "How could he expect to have friends or be invited to parties if he would not allow people to ring his doorbell? And those dogs! I know I'm a dog but some of those guard dogs would even keep me away!"

Then Toby said something that only after he'd said it made him think.

"The giant should knock down the wall, remove the signs and get rid of those dogs. The giant needs to do things different because..." Toby fell silent, thinking.

Cedric and Timothy were attentive. They were beginning to reflect about *their* lives.

Toby muttered under his breath, "The giant needs to do things different."

Christine continued, "Being *responsible* is a spiritual characteristic. It takes seriously the insight that the Rain-God has made us with the gift of being able to make choices. And we are making choices all the time. Even the decision to do nothing is a choice that we are making. The choice NOT to make a choice is still a choice."

"Ha, ha, ha," said Toby. "That's good."

Christine was eager to continue. She was about to sermonize, despite Genesis' cautions, but her audience certainly seemed attentive.

"The giant was making decisions and creating situations that were exactly opposite to what he really wanted in his life. He was creating the pain of loneliness in his life.

"Now it is true that sometimes things happen to us to cause pain that have little to do with our choice or action. But most times, like the giant, we create our own pain."

"Am I c-creating my fear?" said Timothy.

"I'm sure you've asked that question many times, Timothy, and you are still asking the *same* question today. What does that tell us?" asked Christine.

"That it's an unanswerable question," interrupted Toby.

The group became very quiet. Cedric was connecting with Christine and his body started to glow.

"Perhaps when we keep asking a question and not getting an answer we should forget that question and *choose* something else to ask." said Cedric. "Like..."

He was just about to offer a question when Timothy jumped in. "What am I doing t-to move out of my fear?"

"Excellent," said Christine. "You accept the reality of your fear and you make a choice to be responsible for finding ways to move beyond it."

"You did this at the Service of Gratitude, when you confronted your fear, realized that your uniqueness as a snail was loved by the community, and as you sang your song the fear and the stutter went," said Christine.

"B-But it came b-back," said Timothy.

Cedric jumped in. "The Big People have a sacred reading that says something like there can be no fear where there is love. Perfect love casts out fear. This is what I think happened with you, Timothy. You felt loved by the friends at the Service of Gratitude and your fear went away. And it can go again," said Cedric.

"That's right," said Christine. "It can go again when Timothy makes the choice to take a risk. Look at his fears. Be willing to do things differently. And take responsibility for his life."

"That's true for all of us," said Cedric. "I hate to keep going back to this but I was one sad-looking little frog before you dropped into Tunbridge Pond. I was feeling sorry for myself. I had no reason to be miserable but I was *doing* nothing to make my life meaningful. I was hopping around trying to make everyone else happy but I was not taking responsibility for my happiness. In fact, I was on my way to see Mrs. Ramsbottom, in the hope that she could cure my melancholy when you made your now-famous angel-dunk."

They laughed. It was becoming apparent to everyone that you needed a sense of humor if you were to stay in the company of an angel for any length of time. Genesis, on more than one occasion, had told Christine to lighten up.

Toby had stopped licking his wounds and was becoming restless. "Okay. What has this to do with the question you asked me. *Where am I going?*"

"You tell me," said Christine.

"But you're the angel," said Toby. He was not being rude. He just expected angels to have all the answers.

"Become your own angel," said Christine, without skipping a beat.

"Okay, Okay, okay. I think I'm a bit like the giant."

"A b-bit?" said Timothy.

Toby said defensively, "Okay, I'm a lot like the giant. I keep doing the things that create problems in my life and I've not been willing to change them. The giant asked why his life was so miserable. I'm always asking myself why my life is so chaotic, even as I rush off in another direction.

"I know I keep telling people it's not that bad, but the conversation I have within myself is... why do I keep getting into all these messes?'"

"Why do you?" said Cedric.

"Because... I don't really ever take responsibility for what I do. I keep avoiding facing them by saying things aren't that bad. It's my nose and I can't blame other people for where I stick it."

"I need to change my behaviour. I recognize it when I see it in other animals. I hated hearing the terrible things they were saying about Chandu and Chico in the Hay Barn. In fact, I remember asking Muriel, what right did those chickens think they had to be sticking their beaks into other animals' business? That's nothing to do with them!

So instead of always saying it's not that bad, I need to be asking myself what am I prepared to do differently? Why am I in such a hurry? Why don't I ever stay anywhere longer than two minutes?

"I know this isn't the complete answer to those questions but often I'm afraid I'm going to miss something if I don't get moving on down the road. All the time I've been rushing around trying to find that elusive something, I've never once found anything much of interest."

"Why don't you wait until that something finds you?" said Christine.

When Cedric heard Christine say that, something did not set right with him. He hated to disagree with Christine, but he felt there was a better way to help Toby with The Process. He decided to take a risk. "Maybe I could put it another way, if you don't mind, Christine?"

"Go right ahead," suggested Christine. She knew that what Cedric was about to say better expressed what she had intended to say. Well, she thought to herself, I know I'm only an angel in training but I didn't think I'd be instructed by a frog.

As she was thinking this, Genesis popped in. "Remember what I have told you. Everything that lives and breathes carries within it the wisdom of God. Move from your ego into your identity. Even the messages of angels can be improved upon. Yes, even by a seeker frog."

Cedric took a deep breath and concentrated. "Toby, I think that the something that you are rushing to find exists within yourself. All of us tend to think that fun or excitement or meaning exists somewhere other than where we actually are. Christine told me about a famous seeker named Jesus who said that the kingdom exists within each of us. Slow down. And begin to look within."

Christine turned to thank Cedric. To her joy, she saw that they were connected into one glowing circle.

Toby was about to scratch himself when he noticed that his wounds had healed.

Betrayal

Christine felt that the time had come for the celebration supper to take place and so she instructed Cedric, Timothy and Toby to get the word out to their friends.

"Do we have enough time to get ready?" said Cedric.

"Yes," said Christine. "Those who are supposed to be there will be there. Trust me."

"N-Naturally, I'll s-stay here and if any of our friends pass buh-by this way I will surely tell them," said Timothy.

"I'm visiting Old John later and I'll make sure he gets the invitation," said Toby.

"At cock-crow we'll meet at my cottage," said Cedric. "Now I must go off and collect fresh grass, plant-roots and lily leaves... and of course, red berries.

This will be a feast. I'll tell Muriel and she will help me arrange the table."

"While you are all busy making preparations I must go and see somebody who I've not met, and yet I feel I know her very well."

"Do you mean Mabel the goose?" said Toby.

"No, I'm not going to see Mabel the goose. Although I'm sure I will see her sooner rather than later." Christine sometimes said things that sounded dramatic.

Timothy spoke. "M-Mabel the g-goose is part of the g-gossiping chicken trio. I've never really felt at ease with her. She even g-got my nick-name c-confused. Instead of c-calling me Hello-Goodnight she c-called me No Show." The animals laughed.

Christine smiled. She knew she would miss these whimsical times that they had together.

"I'm going to visit Betsy," said Christine.

"Betsy! Betsy the pig!" they all exclaimed.

"Why Betsy?" said Toby. "All she does is lie in that sty of hers and talk to visitors. Don't get me wrong, we all like her. She never does anybody any harm... but then she doesn't do anybody any good."

"I like Buh-Betsy. I feel comfortable in her presence. All the animals feel good when they visit Buh-Betsy," said Timothy.

"We all feel sorry for Betsy," said Cedric. "She is so... so fat. She once nearly flattened me when I went to visit her. She moved unexpectedly. Her hoof almost sent me to frog-Paradise."

"Buh-Betsy moved," said Timothy. "Wow. I know I'm not one t-to talk but I don't th-think I've ever seen Buh-Betsy move. And I've never seen her t-trotters. You n-know — her hooves. When I was little, I thought she moved on her belly like me."

"I'm going to visit Betsy," said Christine. "It is important for me to make *connection* with her. I'll see you all later for the celebration supper."

At that moment Christine hovered maybe three or four feet from the ground and then began to fly in the direction of Olde Stable Farm. She had not gone too far into the cherry orchard that was mid-way between Cedric's cottage and Olde Stable Farm when she felt faint and started losing speed. What was pulling her to the ground?

She landed with a bump in a thicket of dead branches. She was slightly dazed but she could hear in the distance the whispered cluckings of chickens. She climbed onto a dead branch for better vision. It was hard to see exactly who was there but at least twenty animals were gathered for some sort of meeting: a few of the horses, six or more cows, the sheep, Mabel the goose, and Philip the rooster. Alice, Betty and Irma seemed to be leading the meeting and it was Alice's clucking that caught Christine's attention.

"... Teach them a lesson... Nothing good can come... who says she is an angel... devil, more like!... We must get them... best prepared. Remember, get the frog...!"

The animals nodded in agreement and some made whispered comments. Christine could not hear all that was being said, and maybe she did not want to hear. She knew it was connected with the Hay Barn meeting. She knew that Cedric and the other seekers would be tested many times. The Process needed to be played out. This was the beginning of their adventure into the More.

Then an animal slinkily moved to the side of the chickens. His back was towards Christine and so it was hard for her to see exactly who was speaking. But he had the attention of all the animals. Christine strained to hear what was being said. "... Time... give you a sign..." The oily, sleazy voice became more clear. It was Roger. "At the right time I will give you a sign. Then make your move."

Christine felt sick. Although she had expected trouble when she saw Alice, Betty and Irma leave the meeting early, it was still painful to experience. Roger had chosen to move out of The Process. This was the scary aspect of detachment that caused all in Paradise to resist Sophia's eloquent arguments. Detaching meant giving freedom. It seemed to all in Paradise, including THE ONE WHO KNOWS, that whenever the

Celestials detached and left the earth-creatures to their own devices, bad things sometimes happened. (Of course, when *good* things happened, they all applauded the success of The Process!) Still, they grieved when choices led to the path of pain and misery. No one was immune: angels, snakes and ordinary humans had all chosen throughout history to move out of The Process. Now it was Roger's turn to repeat history. The sorrow of it made Christine dizzy.

Christine fell from the branch. Her small body landed amongst the dry leaves, but she was unhurt. Most of the animals at the meeting were so absorbed by the plans being discussed that they were oblivious to the slight noise she created. But Roger had heard it. He fell silent. His cunning and astute instinct told him that somebody was listening.

"Sh. Shh. Everybody be quiet!" he said. "Don't make a sound." Alice, Betty and Irma were looking in all directions. Mabel stretched her neck to see above the thicket of dead branches. Nothing.

Roger got up and moved towards Christine. Instantly Christine covered herself with a few dry leaves. He smelt something. He knew something was there. Roger prided himself on an instinct that was one hundred percent.

Just at the very moment Christine was to be uncovered, a small shrew, nicknamed "Nose" because he had an extremely long nose that he had become very proud of, was passing by looking for food. He had made his home in the thicket of dead branches, preferring life in the country to the crowded existence at Olde Stable Farm. He was friendly with Muriel and had heard about the meeting at the Hay Barn.

"Just stay still. Don't move," Nose instructed.

Roger pounced. "Got you!"

"Well excu-use me. Is this amateur dramatics day?" said Nose. "Are we doing an adventure play that I have not been informed about?"

Roger snarled, annoyed: "What are you doing here?"

"I live here," said Nose. "Have you forgotten, Roger? This is my home. What are *you* doing here?" Looking at the group of animals that were following in the distance, he asked impatiently, "And pray tell me, what are *they* doing here?"

Alice spoke up from the distance. "We are having a meeting. Not to worry. How nice to see you, Nose. It's been a long time since we've seen you at the Gratitude Service."

Nose was known for his dry humor. "I've not had the urge to be grateful for some weeks. When I do feel grateful the Service has usually passed." He then directed his long nose towards Alice, pointedly asking, "Does Mrs. Ramsbottom know about this meeting?"

Roger barked emphatically, "This is a private meeting. It has nothing to do with Mrs. Ramsbottom or Old John or... even you!"

Quickly Nose responded, "But if I'm not mistaken, you came and found me. You crept up on me, nearly scared the wits out of me pouncing on me, and then *you* have the effrontery to imply that I disturbed you? Really!" Nose's nose quivered indignantly.

"Leths continue the meeting," lisped Mabel the goose.

Philip the Rooster, who as we have said was always in a bad temper, shrieked, "We're wasting valuable time!"

Christine could smell Roger's hot breath as she hid behind the leaves. Then there was silence. Roger had gone.

"The coast is clear," said Nose.

Christine sat up and thanked Nose. "What you have done will be remembered," she said appreciatively.

Christine sat on the dry leaves that had been her protection. For a few moments she could not move. She was thinking about betrayal. Why had Roger turned away from his true destiny? His *real* identity? How could he reject the joy that living in The Process would give him? A tear fell from her eye.

Roger was not ready to give up the life that was keeping him disconnected. In a moment of spiritual excitement he had shared with Christine, Cedric and Muriel more than he had intended, making himself vulnerable. Now he was regretting it. Revenge. He needed to remove those animals that knew too much.

"Are you okay?" said Nose.

"No, I'm not okay. But I will be. Let me rest here for a few moments. When that tragic meeting is over I'll have the energy to continue my journey. Thank you, Nose. You just saved an angel!" said Christine.

"Right," said Nose. "That's what I live for!"

They laughed.

Betsy

Christine eventually arrived at the part of Olde Stable Farm that was simply called The Sty. It was a twenty-five foot square concrete block that had been built by Mr. Brown five years ago. And it was built for Betsy.

Betsy had lived at Olde Stable Farm for seven years. Her mother, Rosey, and her brothers and sisters had been sold off years ago. However, nobody wanted the little pig-runt. Mr. Brown's original intention was to fatten her up and when she was into her second year, kill her for Christmas. That never happened. The killing for Christmas. She certainly was fattened up — and up, and up! Indeed, Betsy was probably one of the fattest pigs on the planet. But she was something else. She was unquestionably lovable. Betsy did not have to do anything, she did not have to move a trotter, to get

Big People and animals to love her. Love and friendship came too easily to Betsy. Mr. Brown did not have the heart to serve her up for Christmas lunch. Indeed, Christmas lunch was served up to Betsy. And that is how it had continued for seven long years. Food, followed by food, followed by more food.

When Christine arrived at The Sty, Mabel the goose was also visiting. Everybody loved Betsy and she had more visitors than Mrs. Ramsbottom. However, that did not mean that Betsy approved of all the animals at Olde Stable Farm.

Betsy hated gossip. She was aware that Alice, Betty and Irma, with a group of other animals, including Mabel, had caused problems at the last meeting in the Hay Barn. She was also very fond of Chandu and Chico. Having been the victim of insensitive jokes and unseemly remarks concerning her size she was protective of animals who were also the victims of malicious chit-chat.

She had also been Snake's friend. Indeed, Snake had often spent many hours lying next to Betsy talking about his Snake-disease and feeling a comfort from what he liked to call The Presence. Betsy certainly was a presence. For weeks she had encouraged Snake to eat. But to no avail. She had even asked the Rain-God to take some of her fat and give it to Snake. But the Rain-God had not been inclined to grant her request.

She continued to get fatter, and Snake continued to decline.

Mabel was not one of Betsy's favourite animals. She was a gossip and spreader of tittle-tattle because she wanted to please Alice. She didn't really want to hurt Chandu and Chico, or harm Cedric, or cause upset within the community at Olde Stable Farm, but she was weak. A coward. And she feared what Alice's vicious clucking beak would say about her if she ever disagreed with her.

Mabel had come to see if Betsy agreed with banishing Chandu and Chico from the Farm. Did she approve of their lifestyle? Did she know that they were involved in spreading the horrible Snake-disease that had killed so many animals, not just Snake. Even pigs had died! Would Betsy lend her weight (terrible choice of words!) to the cause of moral purity?

As Christine arrived, Betsy was telling Mabel, in no uncertain terms, that she wanted nothing to do with what she called Hog-Hunting.

"Mabel, tell the friends that sent you over here that I am a friend of Chandu and Chico, and I intend to stay that way! I have always received nothing but kindness from them."

Mabel interrupted, "But they have joined with Cedric to attack Alith and the other chickenth."

"Hog-wash!" said Betsy. I don't believe you. Cedric is no more inclined to attack the chickens than I am to jump this wall. Now lets just stop this Hog-Hunting and do something useful. Let's eat."

At that moment Christine landed on the sty wall.

"Hello my dear. I know who you are. News travels quickly at Olde Stable Farm. You are the angel-friend that is staying with Cedric. How nice of you to come and visit me. And this is... this is Mabel the goose."

"We've met. I know all about Mabel," said Christine.

"Well, I mutht be going. I'll talk with you again, Bet-thy. Don't forget. Think over what I wath telling you," said Mabel.

"I'll not be changing my mind," said Betsy as she chewed an apple.

"I wanted to meet you," said Christine. "I felt it was important for you and me to make a connection."

"Is this angel-speak?" said Betsy. "As you can see, I'm a fat pig whose only pleasure in life is eating, resting and saying hello to visitors. As you will see, I don't even move. Well, very rarely.

"Now, tell me," she continued, "Why would an angel be interested in me?

"Cedric has mentioned you," said Christine. "He did not tell me very much about you..."

"Except that I'm fat," said Betsy. She grinned when she said this. But it was not a convincing grin.

"He did not say very much about you, but when he said your name I felt a positive energy light up my body. Angels know things. We don't know everything. We are not the Rain-God. But we do know some things. And you, Betsy, have something to do."

"What?... What is going on today? Everybody seems to want something from me. First Mabel. And now you! What do you want me to do?"

"I don't know... yet." said Christine. "But I know it is very important."

"Well, you are in for a disappointment," said Betsy. "Didn't anybody tell you? I don't *do* anything. I sit here and eat. Let me make it more clear: Mrs. Ramsbottom doesn't say anything. Timothy doesn't get anywhere. And I don't *do* anything."

Christine laughed.

"I'm an eater," said Betsy. "Some animals talk. Others go on journeys. Some play all day. Others love to organize. Some fight. Many gossip. I eat! That's what I do. That's who I am."

"I don't think so," said Christine. "Let me correct myself. I know that you eat but that is not who you are. You have courage. That is why you condemn gossip and refuse to belong to any clique.

"You embrace diversity. That's why you enjoy Chandu and Chico. You have the gift of intuition. That's how you recognize those who truly are your friends. Oh, yes," said Christine. "You are more than a hog-hamper!"

Betsy laughed. "That's very funny. I'm more than a hog-hamper. Very good."

"Do you agree, "said Christine. "Do you agree that you... you are *more*?"

"Of course. Of course I do when you put it like that," said Betsy.

"How should I put it? Do you really want me to *put it* the way you have been putting it the last seven years?" asked Christine.

"Now don't get too serious with me, little angel, because you don't know me. Not really," said Betsy.

"That may be true. And to be honest, I'm not too interested in finding out all the things that made you become a sedentary food bank."

"Be careful," said Betsy. "Don't make me angry. I don't know what I would do if I became angry."

"Maybe you need to find out. If we could only get beyond the fat into the miracle that exists within you, maybe, just maybe Betsy might become more than a fat joke."

Betsy began to move. "Come here you angelic tick. Come here. What do you mean: maybe I might become more than a fat joke?"

"At this moment that is all that you appear. You appear to be a fat joke that everybody loves. Nobody dislikes you. Nobody disagrees with you. Nobody is irritated by what you say at the meetings because you're never there. Nobody is inspired by what you sing at the Service of Gratitude because you do not attend. "Why? Because you never make your presence *felt*. All you do is sit in this sty and eat. You are becoming what you hate most about yourself. You are becoming a joke!" Christine replied.

"So what. What's wrong with that?" said Betsy.

"Because you are more. You are more than you appear to be... You are *more*."

"Stop saying that. Stop saying..." As she was talking to Christine she was making the effort to stand up. She wanted to speak directly to this irritating angel. With a mighty push and thrust Betsy leaned against the wall to stand up. As she balanced herself on her unstable legs, the side of the wall broke apart. Betsy was left standing in a pile of rubble and Christine was hovering in front of her.

"Now you are free to be whatever you want to be," said Christine.

"What does that mean?" said Betsy.

"Exactly what you want it to mean. You are no longer a prisoner of four square walls that stop you experiencing life on the farm.

"You have been insulated far too long. You have had a protected existence. Why, you didn't have to go out and find friends or food. They came to you. You have been living this way for so long that you actually believed that this was who you were. A hog hamper!

"Now you have a choice. You can crawl back over the rubble and find a corner to rest in. Or you can get out and... live."

Silence enveloped both of them. What a sight: A huge pig standing on a pile of rubble that was once a wall, staring at a hovering angel. By now they were surrounded by animals who had heard the crash as the wall came tumbling down. The animals stared in amazement.

Toby had just finished inviting Old John to the supper with Christine when he heard the crash. He practiced his steady walk — Toby actually walked instead of rushing — down the pathway from the Stables to the Sty to see what was happening.

"Everything okay?" he asked. "Are you okay, Betsy?"

Betsy, who had seen Toby *walk* down the path and had to do a double-take replied, "I'm fine. Are you? What's with this walking? I hardly recognized you!" They smiled at each other.

"I've just been visited by an angel. And I have a feeling my life will never be the same again," continued Betsy.

"I know the feeling," said Toby.

Toby winked at Betsy. "Long as you're up, why don't you join us for our feast? Seems you lost your dinner under all that rubble."

Betsy surveyed the ruins. "Perhaps I shall."

The Last Supper

Cedric and Muriel busied themselves preparing the supper that Christine had requested. The fresh grass was indeed fresh; they had plant-roots and lily leaves in abundance and there were enough red berries for everyone. Cedric and Muriel usually worked well together once Cedric made the decision to leave the organization to Muriel. Toby had also arrived early to offer his newly acquired steady and reliable services.

Considering the short notice the seekers had been given, all had indicated that they would be arriving at Cedric's cottage by cock-crow.

Christine had made the difficult decision not to say anything about the betrayal of Roger.

She had no doubt that Roger would attend the supper and would be his usual charming self . Only *she* would know the truth.

Christine had spent the time before the supper meditating with Genesis. More than ever she needed to be in touch with the Spiritual Principles of Insight, Wisdom and Harmony. She also wanted to reconnect with Genesis. As her prime sponsor, he helped her to strengthen her connection to The Process. The preparation time had been beneficial; she was feeling a glow at the center of her being.

At the time that nature had predetermined, the cock crew. Everything was ready. Cedric, Muriel and Toby were standing near the table of goodies. Muriel was fantasizing about the flavour of plant-roots. Toby was concentrating on remaining calm.

Cedric had a mixture of feelings going on within himself. He knew that very soon he would be saying good-bye to Christine and although she said that she would spiritually always be with him, that is not what he wanted. He wanted to see her. He wanted to feel her beautiful body. He knew, and he knew that she knew, he had fallen in love with an angel. He pondered if the poet was right who had said it was better to have loved and lost than never to have loved at all.

Cedric also sensed danger. Something about this supper disturbed him. He did not feel relaxed, even though he would soon be eating red berries with Christine and his dear friends. The feeling of hop-lessness was returning. Disconnection was in the air.

He was thinking these things when he heard the sound of somebody knocking, very gently at the door. He was hopping to answer it when Christine appeared at his side. "Do not be afraid. Everything is going to be okay. Do you believe me?"

"Yes, I believe you," said Cedric. "But something does not feel right."

Again, Christine repeated herself. "Do not be afraid. Everything is going to be okay. Believe me?"

"I do, but still..." said Cedric.

"All that will happen is necessary. Do you believe that?"

"I believe in you," said Cedric, and the beginnings of a tear appeared in his eye.

Another gentle knock was heard at the door. Toby, practicing developing his sensitivity, said that he would get it. When he opened the door nobody was there. Strange, he thought.

He was just about to close the door when Timothy squealed, "D-don't c-close the d-door! You'll squash me! I'm halfway in. G-give me a few more minutes... wh-what t-took you s-so long?"

"You told me not to be in such a hurry," said Toby. "When I do what you suggest you still complain!" He then impersonated a famous announcer. "LADIES AND GENTLEFROG. IT GIVES ME GREAT

PLEASURE TO ANNOUNCE THE ARRIVAL OF OUR FIRST GUEST. HELLO-GOODNIGHT HAS FINALLY ARRIVED!"

"And how are you going to announce a dog's two best friends?" It was the unmistakable purr of Chandu and Chico.

Not missing a beat, Toby continued, "LADIES AND GENTLECREATURES, TO ADD THE INTERNATIONAL FLAVOUR — DARE I SAY SPICE — TO THIS EVENING, WELCOME THE INSEPARABLE CHANDU AND CHICO!"

Chandu and Chico looked impeccable, wearing matching lavender collars with gold hanging bells. Understatement was their trademark, except when it came to showing affection.

The animals processed in a line to the table that was positioned in the center of the room. There they were ceremoniously greeted by Christine, Cedric and Muriel. No sooner had Toby closed it than Old John banged on the door.

"LADIES AND GENTLECREATURES. GIVE IT UP FOR THE SENIOR RESIDENT OF OLDE STABLE FARM, WHO WAS, AND IS, AND EVER SHALL BE."

Toby was getting tired. He wished he'd never started this dramatic announcing, but now that he had started he could hardly stop — without hurting the feelings of late arrivers.

Muriel asked Cedric, "Who else are we expecting?"

"Let me see," said Cedric. "John's here... Timothy...we are only waiting for Roger and Betsy."

"Buh-Betsy will never arrive," said Timothy. "She's not w-walked for years."

"I think Hello-Goodnight is right. I'll perform a back-flip if she ever arrives," said Muriel. Everybody laughed.

"I've never seen a hedgehog back-flip," said Christine cryptically. Everybody became attentive. Did Christine know something that they didn't?

"Make sure you hold your quills down when you flip or you'll spike yourself to death!" laughed Cedric.

Muriel was not amused.

A furtive scratching on the door created an eerie silence. The animals all looked at each other. Christine felt queasy. She knew it was Roger.

"Only me. Sorry to be late but I had some business to attend. Good to see you all." The insincerity was oozing out of him but all the animals as usual were charmed.

"Stop!" said Toby. "You must be announced! LADIES AND GENTLECREATURES. NOW I PRESENT ROGER TO YOU

A NATURAL CHARMER — A SLY ONE, TOO!
BUT ON MEETING AN ANGEL

HE FOUND HIS TRUE REASON
AND NOW HE'S A FRIEND FOR ALL
SEASONS!"

The animals applauded Toby's 'verse-atility.'

"Thank you so much," said Roger. "I wished I'd been here for your previous announcements. Turning to find Christine in the room, he said in sugared tones, "Nice to see you, Christine."

Then Roger did something unusual. He greeted Cedric with a kiss. "My dear friend. I'm honored to be in your home."

Awkward silence engulfed the gathering. Something did not feel right.

After a moment Muriel took charge. "Now everybody, we need to take our places for the supper. This is a farewell to Christine, and we cannot say goodbye without eating plant-roots."

The animals laughed. Muriel hadn't realized that she was being funny. She laughed anyway. The awkwardness was beginning to lift.

Muriel bustled about, getting everyone settled. "You will see that we have arranged place cards for where you are to sit. Please do not complain or try to change the cards.

"Also, the arrangement is at the request of Christine. We will all be sitting at one side of the table, with the exception of Chandu and Roger, who will sit on the corners."

Muriel caught herself being bossy. She immediately breathed in and relaxed. "Let's enjoy."

Christine was aware that Muriel battled with herself as she sought to detach, and was glowingly proud. Christine also realized she had not interfered, but had let Muriel find her own way. Genesis would be beaming. So would Sophia!

It truly was a feast. The table was stacked with vegetables and fruit that all the animals enjoyed. There was enough for everyone... and more. Remember, Christine expected Betsy.

"Where could she be?" Christine wondered to herself.

Toby, Muriel and Old John were about to dig in when Christine hovered above the table, commanding attention.

"This is a feast of friendship. We meet as a community of seekers. Forever our lives will be connected. Before we eat I would like to bless the food and our lives, in gratitude for The Process that brought us together."

Chico whispered to Chandu. "What does she mean?"

"Shh," said Chandu. "I don't know what she means. We've not spent enough time with her. But I feel a strong connection with her. It's not what she says, it's the way she makes me feel," he smiled at Chico.

"I know," said Chico. "I feel it, too."

Christine spoke, glowing ever brighter, "We embrace the friendship that we are creating in this place. We are seekers. We are challenged to become the healers we were intended to be. This is The Process. We bless this food that is symbolic of our shared destiny. This we accept."

Christine then took a moment to look at all the faces gathered around the table. When she came to Roger she stared lovingly. He looked away.

"C-Can we eat? I'm really hungry. It t-took me forever to g-get here," said Timothy, breaking the uncomfortable silence.

Christine looked around the table. "Enjoy. And remember."

The food was excellent. It had the taste of… more. Although the food was familiar it seemed different. Cedric started to think about honey. "I wonder if this is what honey tastes like?" he thought.

The animals had moved all around the table and were enjoying themselves. Christine particularly stayed close to Cedric and Timothy. She wanted them to feel a special relationship with her.

Roger came and brought Christine a red berry. "This is for you, Christine. I hope you never forget me."

"How could I ever forget you. Whenever this evening is spoken about your role will be remembered," said Christine.

The Gifts

Then Christine hovered above the table to make an announcement. "Now we will give each other a gift."

"Oh, d-dear. I only b-brought myself," stuttered Timothy.

"The gift I am talking about is spiritual. It will help all of us live The Process," said Christine. "I want you to turn to the friend seated next to you and give them a word — only one word — but the word you give is the word that person needs to hear.

"Words are not just descriptions of things. They have an energy within them. The word that you speak reflects a unique energy."

"How does this work?" asked Cedric.

"You will see," said Christine. "Let me begin with you Cedric. I will give you the gift of a word and after you have received it, you will then turn and give a word gift to John. John will then turn and give a word-gift to

Roger, who will then move and give the gift to Chandu. So it goes."

"Oh, g-goody," said Timothy. He was beginning to glow with excitement.

Christine then turned to Cedric. The room became deafeningly silent. "The word I give you is... Perseverance."

Cedric, feeling a deep connection with Christine, knew this word would be required in the future.

"Thank you," Cedric said. Then Cedric turned to John. Without a moment's hesitation he knew the word that John needed to hear. "I give you the gift of... Forgiveness."

John gruffly repeated the word. "Forgiveness... Hmm..." Within himself he knew that the word truly was for him — John needed to forgive himself. He was still holding on to his past mistakes, especially those concerning Elizabeth. John then moved past Betsy's empty place to Roger.

"This seems rather silly," said Roger. However, the seriousness with which John approached him soon removed his grin.

"Roger, I give you the gift of... Integrity." Roger accepted the gift with a nod. He was thinking as he moved towards Chandu what his word might mean. He dismissed further consideration. It was too late now. The trap had already been set.

The sickly grin returned to Roger's face. "The gift I give you is... Joy."

"Thank you," said Chandu. Everybody in the room was now smiling with Chandu. Joy was certainly a word that had resonated in his life... long may it continue.

Chandu turned towards Chico. "My gift to you is... Commitment."

"Thank you, my dearest," said Chico, kissing Chandu on both cheeks as if bestowing a medal. Chico was always a wee bit melodramatic. He closed his eyes and brought his paws together in a prayer position. Nothing was said. Then he opened his eyes instantly and looked directly at Toby. "Patience. My gift to you is Patience."

Toby thought to himself, "Has somebody been talking with him?" But he said nothing. Deliberately he thanked Chico. Equally deliberately, without fuss, he turned to face Muriel.

"I give you the gift of... Acceptance."

Muriel knew that was *her* word. She needed to accept the way the life is rather than how she wanted it to be. "Thank you," said Muriel.

The gift-giving created a solemnity rarely shared by the group. Christine sensed that the animals were not just listening to the words being shared but they were digesting what their word meant for them. That was the purpose of the exercise. Christine knew that there was no magic attached to the words themselves. The real magic came with the creative effort and energy that would be used to make the words come alive. Connection. One thing Christine knew, this group of seekers would take their words into the adventures that awaited them.

"My t-turn!" said Timothy.

"Wait!" said Muriel.

"Is that my word? *Wait*? Please, Rain-God, say it isn't so," said Timothy. All the animals laughed.

"Shh. Shh. My word to you is... Courage." Muriel smiled at Timothy.

Timothy extended his neck beyond his shell. "Yes. Yes. Thank you, Muriel."

Everyone looked at Christine expectantly. What word would Timothy give to Christine? How could a snail give anything to an Angel?

"M-my gift to you... and I don't know why I am saying this... I hope you d-don't get mad with me... but the word is in my mind... Trust!"

Christine knew the importance of this word. On many occasions, Genesis had had to remind Christine to *trust* The Process... trust in the long term goal rather than the quick fix. Christine thanked Timothy and gently kissed him on the neck. The she turned and looked at Roger... Trust.

"Shall we take some air?" asked Roger jauntily. "Let's take our gifts out into the night."

"You can't be serious?" remarked Chico.

"It's too dangerous... too many insects," said Toby, rubbing his butt.

"Okay, Roger. We can go out for a few moments. Lead the way," said Christine.

It seemed strange. Awkward. Uncomfortable. Although it did not feel right, everyone followed Christine and Roger into the night.

They had not gone too far when Roger turned and said, "Let's play a game."

"A game?" asked Cedric. "Are you serious?"

"Yes, yes I am. And you are going to be the main player. I suggest — leap-frog."

"Leap-frog?" said Cedric. "That's what little Big People play. No frog would ever play leap-frog."

"Until tonight," said Roger. "You stay down and I'll jump over you. But go further out into the field. So that I can take a long run and jump over you... Go on, Cedric. Go further out into the field."

"Do what he says," said Christine.

It was an odd sight. Christine and the other animals had formed a group, Roger had separated himself about six feet from the other animals and poor little Cedric was hopping out — alone — into the field. Night had fallen.

"Okay, you can stop. You can stop, Cedric," said Roger. Then Roger lifted his head to the moon and gave a haunting fox-cry. Everybody froze. Including Cedric, who was now twenty feet from the security of his fellow seekers.

"Look!" said Toby. "Who are they?" Eyes appeared all around Cedric. Because it was night it was hard to see shapes, but Cedric was surrounded by eyes.

A clucking shriek pierced the air. "Let's get him!" Suddenly a pointy beak stabbed into Cedric's leg and threw him in the air. Sharp teeth grabbed his body, hurling him sideways into a pair of powerful jaws that snapped him up and pitched him high into the sky. He landed with a sickening thud near a hoof that batted him across the field. Poor Cedric. Animals were picking him up and tumbling him in all directions.

John and Toby were about to move, when a group of animals led by Philip the rooster surrounded them.

"Don't make a move, John," said Philip. "Stay still. And you too, Toby."

The seekers were clearly confused and taken by surprise. One of the younger mules bit the side of John's neck to reinforce the point: this was no game.

Muriel screamed, "Watch your back. Enemies in the camp. Enemies, I say!"

Christine hovered above Cedric's head. She summoned up all her energy and within seconds made time stand still. Everything stopped. Now, what should she do?"

Genesis spoke to her. "Detach. Do nothing. Trust. Remember that word, Christine? Trust The Process."

"But they are killing Cedric!" said Christine.

"Trust... trust The Process," said Genesis. Immediately, he was gone.

"Trust!" she screamed. Tears were running down her cheeks. "Then let time begin!"

The attack on Cedric resumed. All that the seekers could do was watch, helplessly.

Roger walked over and joined the attackers. "Don't kill him. Just shake him up."

He looked into Cedric's eyes. Cedric was bleeding and disoriented. All he could mutter was, "Why, Roger. Why?"

Roger picked Cedric up in his teeth, shook him and then threw him to the ground. He only intended to put the fear of the Rain-God into Cedric, and he wanted the others to help scare Cedric into going away.

"Take your friendth and go. Go away from Tunbridge Pond. Go!" Mabel the goose honked, following Alice, Betty and Irma who were shrieking and clucking wildly.

"Go! Go away from Tunbridge Pond."

A huge animal suddenly lunged out of the shadows and charged the attacking mules, then it head-butted Roger.

"Take that!"

The head then swung around and side-swiped the chickens and Mabel the goose. "And that! Take that!" Alone, the huge animal faced the twenty or more animals that surrounded poor Cedric. "Who's next?"

It was Betsy.

The seekers that had been surrounded suddenly broke through their guards. "Let's get them!" Toby cried.

"Come. Let's follow Toby. And please, my dear, stay close to me," said Chandu to Chico.

"Bite me again and I'll break your neck," said John to the young mule who was still standing guard.

"I'm with you, John," said Muriel.

"S-So am I. S-So am I!" squeaked Timothy bravely.

Betsy then walked over to Cedric. She licked the blood and dirt from his body.

"Don't worry. You'll be fine." Then Betsy turned her fierce gaze to Roger.

"You silly fox. Now collect your friends and get out of here before I do some real damage. Go!"

Roger began backing away. Alice, Betty and Irma, together with Mabel and the remaining animals, began retreating with him. Within seconds they had gone.

The seekers moved quickly to comfort Cedric. Then John began to sing.

Feel the stillness growing, in each and every heart.
See the love-glow shining, never to depart.
We are ONE together, knowing we are free.
Let it be. Let it be.

All the animals joined in. Christine hovered above them. She murmured, "Thank you, Genesis. Trust. They are becoming their own angels."

Cedric gingerly turned to Muriel, grinning mischievously. "Ready for your back-flip, Muriel?" Everybody laughed.

Mrs. Ramsbottom, who lived deep in the forest, saw a bright glow coming from the field near Cedric's cottage. "I have a feeling that this place will never be the same again." Then she blinked.

Genesis and Sophia

Mrs. Ramsbottom smelled incense and knew she was not alone. Genesis sat on the branch next to her.

"It's been a long time, Sophia. I hardly recognized you behind all those feathers." As Genesis spoke, he fidgeted on the branch, trying discreetly to find a comfortable place to rest his posterior. He'd chosen to take the form of a little Big Person for his visit with Sophia.

"After more than three thousand years, I see you're still trying to accommodate yourself," Sophia observed tartly as Genesis continued to squirm. Eventually Genesis found comfort sitting on his hands, which made a rather bony cushion. He immediately lost balance again the first time he removed his hand to pull his earring.

"I swear, Sophia, we meet in the strangest places!"

Sophia gazed at Genesis from behind her huge owl eyes. She'd always enjoyed his eccentric manner. "How are you, old friend?" she smiled.

"Busy." His raspy voice brought back fond memories of working together with some of the greatest seekers.

"I had a feeling you'd show up when I spotted Whatsername — Christine. I sensed she was one of yours. Interesting. She has great potential if she could only learn to shut up, keep out of the way and let The Process work." Sophia knew that she was getting on her soapbox. "I know, I know. I'm singing that tired old song again."

"She's getting it," rasped Genesis.

Sophia continued, "Let's put it this way — and I mean no offense — " Genesis knew she was about to launch a verbal barb. "For an angelic side-kick, she got it a lot quicker than her unusual, dare I say outlandish, mentor. With the earring and before the earring. She most certainly got it faster than YOU KNOW WHO!"

Timidly, Genesis murmured, "You mean, THE ONE WHO KNOWS?"

"Exactly," said Sophia. "Anyway, I'm not here to tell you I told you so. But I did! The Process only makes sense if we practice detachment. Otherwise, we've gone right back to priestly tricksters, charlatans and a fix-it religion."

"We agree. We agree. No argument. It just took time for us to comprehend the spiritual distinction between detachment and disconnection. You know THE ONE WHO KNOWS has always had difficulty, right from the beginning of creation, loving from a distance."

Sophia suddenly became serious. "Why are you here?"

Genesis fidgeted more than ever, pulling his earring and nervously coughing.

"THE ONE WHO KNOWS would like you to return. You would not have to reapply. Just say the word. We miss you. We need you. Insight and Wisdom, we have in abundance, but we really need you to bring Harmony.

"Would you detach yourself back into being an Archangel? There are worse things you could be! I'm sure you didn't enjoy being a monkey in Asia."

Sophia interrupted. "I was a gorilla, not a monkey. And it was Africa. "

Genesis smiled. He loved to play these games with her. "What about it, Sophia. You've made your point." He could not quite bring himself to say THE ONE WHO KNOWS *hadn't* known everything.

He continued. "Your work is done here. We all need to detach and let Cedric and the other seekers embrace The Process and create their own adventures."

Genesis sensed that Sophia was downcast. It is hard to recognize melancholy in the face of an owl, but he knew that although she championed detachment, she struggled with pulling away and moving on. Even for Archangels, The Process is easier to talk about than live!

He pressed on. "I know you'll miss these creatures. I'm beginning to miss them myself and I don't even know them. But it's time to move on."

"After the miracle that your sidekick has performed around here, I suppose you're right," mused Sophia. "It's time for me to move on."

"You know, Genesis, the hardest part of our work is having to keep moving on. It really hurts. I know I'm going to miss the animals, especially my dear friend Rebecca. I rather like the simplicity of being an animal among animals. Oh, well..."

Genesis looked softly into her eyes. "Will you take your old job back? We really need you."

Flapping her wings and turning her head in all directions, Sophia cooed, "Why not? If THE ONE WHO KNOWS is ready for me, then I'm ready for the O-W-K!" Her eyes sparkled. "I have some ideas about interplanetary connection, developing a Harmony with life forms in other solar systems. A new age is dawning and we'd better be prepared."

Genesis grinned broadly and rasped his farewell. "See you in Paradise!" He was gone before the words left his lips, leaving only a lingering wisp of incense.

Sophia smiled after him, stretching her wings. She did so enjoy the sensations of her owl body. She plumped her bosom, rotated her head three times, and became again the sagely formidable Mrs. Ramsbottom. "Yes, I have a feeling this place will never be the same again." Then she blinked.

Good-bye

All the animals stayed the night at Cedric's cottage, talking until the early morning about what they should do to avenge the attack on Cedric.

"I think we should call a special meeting," said Chandu.

"They cannot be allowed to get away with this," said Chico.

"No animal is safe," said Muriel. "They're worse than strangers in the camp. The traitor has shown his face."

Cedric, who was beginning to recover his strength, tried to get a word in edgewise. "I think we should seek to teach what we have learned from Christine." He turned to her. "Maybe you could stay and help us?"

Christine smiled, glowing bright yellow. "All the time I have been with you I only reflected back to you what you already knew deep within yourselves. You are more than capable of continuing your adventures using the Spiritual Principles of Harmony, Insight and

Wisdom. Remember, you are now the seekers. Trust The Process."

"I think we should call a meeting and banish Roger and the gossiping trio," said John.

"Remember the word I gave you," said Cedric. "It was a gift to you, John, but you can offer it to others."

John thought about his word: Forgiveness. Never did he expect to share his gift with a foxy traitor and a gang of chickens.

The animals knew that Cedric was right. Revenge is never the answer. Also, they sensed that revenge is not a characteristic of The Process.

"Do you have anything to eat?" said Betsy.

"Oh, yes," said Muriel. "We have some fresh grass, red berries, lily leaves and... wait for it... plant-roots."

"What about potatoes and bread?" asked Betsy, in the meekest tone she could muster.

"Sorry," said Muriel.

"Oh, well. I suppose I'll embrace the concept of change. Fresh vegetables. AAGGHH!"

Everyone laughed.

"Betsy, that could be your word," said Timothy. "Change." Timothy turned to Christine. "Is it okay to choose your own word, Christine? Can you give yourself a gift-word?"

"They are the best gifts. The gifts that we give ourselves," said Christine.

"Okay," said Betsy. "I think I know what you are talking about, so I'll embrace the word Change."

Chandu and Chico had been licking each other during most of the conversation but their ears, simultaneously, had become attentive when Timothy had spoken.

"Timothy! Timothy!" they exclaimed. "You are not stuttering. Good Rain-God, Timothy, you are not stuttering!"

Timothy looked around the group. Amazed he exclaimed, "That's right. I'm not stuttering. I'm willing to face my fears. That takes... Courage. My word. Thank you, Muriel. You gave me the word I needed to hear."

Muriel moved forward and kissed Timothy. Everybody felt connected.

All the seekers were laughing and sharing all that they had learned together. John was telling Betsy about the benefits of plant-roots. Muriel was discussing with Timothy, Chandu and Chico how she was going to accept life at Olde Stable Farm and Tunbridge Pond rather than try to stage-manage everybody. Toby was practicing Patience in the corner. Christine signaled to Cedric it was time to go.

"Come," she said in a quiet voice that only he could hear. Unnoticed they went through the door and in silence Cedric followed Christine to Tunbridge Pond.

They went down to the oak branch that stretched across the Pond casting its welcoming shadow.

"This is where it all began," said Cedric.

"This is where it will begin," said Christine.

"I know why I needed to be with you. And now *you* know. You were hoping for an angel to come and make everything okay. Well, you got your angel. He's a frog. Or a hedgehog, or a cat, or a dog, or a mule ... yes, one day, even a fox! Don't misunderstand me. I know I'm training to be an angel — one who brings the message, but the Spiritual Principles that lead to The Process are about discovering the message in the living of our lives."

"Will I ever see you again?" asked Cedric.

"I will always be with you," said Christine. "When you really need me I will make my presence known. And you will know it is me.

"Now, join the other seekers and let the adventure begin."

Cedric closed his eyes and puckered his lips to give Christine a farewell kiss. His experienced a glow deep within him and then a cool breeze made its presence felt. He opened his eyes and Christine was gone.

As he was hopping back to his cottage, a lady mule passed him heading in the direction of Olde Stable Farm. It was Elizabeth.

But that's another story.

LEO BOOTH

He's a different kind of priest who says you don't have to be religious to be spiritual. The dynamic Englishman is a spiritual 'rebel with a cause': He wants to bring spirituality back into religion, and help everyone discover that spirituality is simply the essence of being real and human. An energetic mix of Charlie Chaplin with a touch of Dudley Moore, he's an Episcopal priest who's as likely to quote *The Velveteen Rabbit* as often as the Bible. He's not afraid to tweak the noses of religious and psychotherapy establishments to get his message across, but once he's heard, he treats his listeners with warmth, dignity, compassion and insight.

For over 20 years he has focused on helping people reclaim their spiritual power. A recovering alcoholic and certified addictions and eating disorders counselor, he is a national consultant to treatment programs and organizations. Rev. Booth is an active Episcopal priest in the Diocese of Los Angeles. *The Angel and The Frog* is his sixth book.

BOOKS BY LEO BOOTH

THE ANGEL AND THE FROG
In this charming spiritual fable, Cedric the Frog and the residents of Olde Stable Farm meet an angel named Christine and discover the Spiritual Process.
SCP Limited

THE GOD GAME — IT'S YOUR MOVE:
Reclaim Your Spiritual Power
We don't "get" spiritual. Our spirituality is built into us at creation, in the connection between Mental, Physical and Emotional. Claiming our spiritual power involves connecting to ourselves and learning to make our spiritually powerful moves.
Stillpoint Publishing

WHEN GOD BECOMES A DRUG:
Breaking the Chains of Religious Addiction and Abuse
This challenging and insightful look at the symptoms and sources of religious addiction and abuse is also a guide to attaining healthy spirituality.
Putnam\Perigee

SAY YES TO LIFE: Daily Meditations
365 daily meditations on issues relating to alcoholism, chemical dependency, eating disorders and codependency.
SCP Limited

MEDITATIONS FOR COMPULSIVE PEOPLE
In this collection of meditations in verse, Leo the poet meets Leo the theologian. Revised, with worksheet and process questions.
SCP Limited

SPIRITUALITY AND RECOVERY
One of the most popular of Father Leo's works, this book is a guide to creating healthy spirituality in recovery. It explains the difference between religion and spirituality, and suggests ways in which to become a positive, creative person
SCP Limited

OTHER MATERIALS

40 INDIVIDUAL AUDIOS
and AUDIO ALBUMS (4 titles per set)

Individual audios and album sets on spirituality, religious abuse, self-empowerment, drug and alcohol abuse, codependency, relationship and life issues.

VIDEOS

An excellent addition to your recovery library, especially for treatment programs, hospitals, alcohol and drug councils. Each approximately 55 minutes running time.

V1	Say Yes To Life
V2	Meditations For Compulsive People
V3	Spirituality and Adult Children of Alcoholics Recovery
V4	Creating Healthy Relationships
V5	Recovery From An Eating Disorder
V6	Intervention: Creating an Opportunity to Live
V7	Overcoming Religious Addiction and Religious Abuse
V8	An Evening With Father Leo

ANNUAL SPIRITUAL EMPOWERMENT
CONFERENCE CRUISES AND RETREATS

Each year, Leo Booth presents conference cruises and retreats. During these fun-filled days, you'll explore all aspects of healthy spirituality, from the morning "Attitude of Gratitude" meeting to the evening dancing and play. Themes include manifesting your life's dreams, achieving goals, claiming spiritual power and healing spiritual wounds of addictions or other issues. Dates and itineraries vary from year to year. Space is limited and fills up quickly, so early reservations are recommended.

CONFERENCES * WORKSHOPS INSERVICES
* CONSULTANCIES

Leo Booth works with a variety of groups and organizations, from treatment centers and therapists, to the general public, teaching how to create healthy spirituality. The Spiritual Concepts staff will help you with any phase of the event, from choosing a topic to suggesting marketing strategies and creating ads and copy. If you would like to share his wit, wisdom and zest for life with your program or organization call Spiritual Concepts at (800) 284-2804.

FOR A COMPLETE CATALOG AND OTHER INFORMATION CALL:

Spiritual Concepts
(800) 284-2804
(8:00 AM - 4:00 PM Pacific time Monday - Friday)
2700 St. Louis Avenue
Long Beach, CA 90806

Internet: www.fatherleo.com
E-Mail: frleo@deltanet.com